The Real World of Ideology

HARVESTER PHILOSOPHY NOW

General Editor: ROY EDGLEY, *Professor of Philosophy, University of Sussex*

English-speaking philosophy since the Second World War has been dominated by linguistic analysis, the latest phase of the analytical movement started in the early years of the century.

As our twentieth-century world has staggered from crisis to crisis, English-speaking philosophy in particular has submissively dwindled into a humble academic specialism on its own understanding, isolated from substantive issues in other disciplines, from the practical problems facing society, and from contemporary Continental thought.

The books in this series are united by discontent with this state of affairs. Convinced that the analytical movement has spent its momentum, its latest phase – perhaps its last – the series seeks in one way or another to push philosophy out of its ivory tower.

The Real World
of Ideology

JOE McCARNEY

Senior Lecturer in Philosophy, Polytechnic of the South Bank

HARVESTER PRESS·SUSSEX

HUMANITIES PRESS·NEW JERSEY

First published in Great Britain in 1980 by
THE HARVESTER PRESS LIMITED
Publishers: John Spiers and Margaret A. Boden
16 Ship Street, Brighton, Sussex

and in the USA by
HUMANITIES PRESS INC.,
Atlantic Highlands, New Jersey 07716

© Joe McCarney, 1980

British Library Cataloguing in Publication Data
McCarney, Joe
    The real world of ideology. – (Philosophy now; 9).
    1. Ideology   2. Communism
    I. Title   II. Series
    145   B823.3

    ISBN 0-85527-866-8
        0-85527-438 7 (pbk)

Humanities Press Inc.
ISBN 0-391-01704-7
        0-391-01705-5 (pbk)

Printed and bound in Great Britain by
Redwood Burn Limited, Trowbridge and Esher

CONTENTS

PREFACE

This essay is a study of the treatment of ideology by Marxist thinkers. The topic has a life outside that context, and issues of great interest have been raised there. Nevertheless, there is a case for regarding its place within it as crucial for the debate as a whole. Marx is usually acknowledged as, historically, the most important influence in the field, with the main responsibility for introducing the notion into general intellectual currency. Moreover, his work continued to shape its fortunes thereafter, in that later writers have felt obliged to define their position in relation to what they take to be his, whether in order to support or attack it. This in itself, of course, would not justify yet another discussion of a well-worn theme. For that one has to rely on a claim which the body of the essay will seek to substantiate, that the character of the Marxist tradition in this area is now generally misunderstood by friendly and hostile commentators alike. The failure has a radical aspect: it is rooted in a mistaken view of the nature of the conception of ideology held by Marx and the classical Marxist thinkers. Hence, the first chapter will be concerned to explicate that conception. The next two chapters will pursue the argument in relation to the main lines of misconceived development in the later period. The final chapter will try to locate the theme of ideology within the overall pattern of the historical development of Marxist thought.

There are some debts that should be acknowleged here. The first is to Dr Otto Newman, Head of the Department of Social Sciences, Polytechnic of the South Bank, for his consistent encouragement of this project, and in particular for its practical expression in arranging the measure of relief from teaching responsibilities that facilitated its completion. My thanks are due to a number of colleagues for their co-operation in this, and most of all to Dick de Zoysa who had to bear the brunt of the inconvenience that resulted. I should like to add that it was the experience of planning and teaching a course with him that led to my serious interest in the questions discussed in this book

I am indebted to Nick Worrall for confirming that the standard translations of Lenin could be relied on to the extent I required.

I am grateful most of all to Roy Edgely, General Editor of the 'Philosophy Now' series. He has read the entire manuscript in draft, and his detailed comments have been very helpful in preparing the final version. I also attach considerable importance to his interest in the project at an early and difficult stage of its development.

Finally, I wish to record my sense of the incalculable debt I owe my wife for her support throughout the period of writing this book.

JOE MCCARNEY

CHAPTER 1

MARX'S CONCEPTION

SOME preliminary remarks should be made about the method of inquiry to be used in this chapter. The task of explicating Marx's view of ideology is one which, notoriously, gets no systematic attention in his own writings. Indeed, for all the use made of the concept there is little that may safely be taken even by way of oblique comment on its grammar. We are given a set of clues and left to discover the pattern for ourselves. Here is a central fact of his procedure, and one must come to terms with it. The reticence of the texts has to be respected as a true reflection of the nature of his interests in this area. These are overwhelmingly conjunctural and instrumental, scarcely ever taking a turn towards analysis or general reflection. The problems that result will be familiar enough to students of what Antonio Gramsci has called 'a conception of the world which has never been systematically expounded by its founder'.[1] The founder's treatment of ideology might have been designed to point up this description, and in the circumstances some degree of methodological austerity seems advisable. At any rate this discussion will concentrate initially on the explicit references to ideology and the ideological to be found in Marx's work: these are the primary clues that have to be fitted together. It will be assumed that where he wishes to use the concept he will generally be prepared to do so under its own name. The inquiry will then be directed to reconstructing the principle of this usage. It will ask what it presupposes, what general assumptions it is shaped by and what view of the nature of ideology can best make sense of it.

The decision to develop one's account of a concept on the

basis of the clear-cut instances of its use may seem uncontentious and indeed scarcely worth stating. In the case of most major thinkers this might well be so. It does not generally seem to occur to interpreters of Locke on 'primary and secondary qualities' or Wittgenstein on 'family resemblance' to set about their task in any other way, and there is no reason why Marx should not be shown the same respect. The exegesis of his work has, nevertheless, its own distinctively relaxed traditions. The proposal made here would in fact be hard to square with much of what currently passes for discussion of his views on ideology. The standard weakness of this literature is an insensitivity to its subject-matter, a failure to respond to the pressure of its concrete details. The varied ways in which the tendency manifests itself will be documented in the later course of the discussion. It is mentioned here to lend point to the suggestion that in this area a certain dryness may now be in order. Such an emphasis has its familiar risks of scholasticism and the fetishism of the quotation, of being overwhelmed by details or of treating them with a literalness that misses the spirit entirely. But no such fate is inevitable. It may help to bear in mind the rules of method which Gramsci prescribed for himself in this kind of situation. He lays due stress on the importance of what he calls 'preliminary detailed philological work' to be carried out 'with the most scrupulous accuracy, scientific honesty and intellectual loyalty and without any preconceptions, apriorism or *parti pris*'.[2] But the advice is to be taken in conjunction with the later warning: 'Search for the *Leitmotiv,* for the rhythm of the thought as it develops, should be more important than that for single casual affirmations and isolated aphorisms.'[3] The guiding assumption of this discussion is that a sense of the *Leitmotiv* is best developed out of attention to detail. It must be recognized, however, that unless such a general understanding is achieved all the preliminary detailed work is in vain. Moreover, once established it need not be permanently confined to the range of instances from which it was built up in the first place. Thus, it should be possible to apply it to phenomena of which Marx could have had no experience, to draw out implications he never considered and, with due caution, to use it in exploring the silences and lacunae of the texts. For if the original insight is incapable of this kind of organic development it can have little permanent interest or value.

Such a programme might, of course, be doomed to fail through some defect in the raw material; if, for instance, it should be the case that Marx's usage is informed by no consistent themes but is irredeemably arbitrary or incoherent. This would be a disappointing conclusion, but there is no need to assume it at the start. Indeed, one might have a rational hope that it will turn out not to be so. His distinctive quality as a thinker lies not in any special taste for abstract theorizing but in the ability to handle masses of detail within a single focus of vision, and to assign particulars unerringly to their place in the light of it. The task of this chapter is to uncover the principle of such judgments for the category of ideology. As soon as one starts to work on it, such misgivings as have been raised tend to vanish. The 'rhythm' of his thought in this area turns out to be remarkably insistent and regular, and this, to anticipate a little further, is because it is tuned to the heart-beat of the system as a whole. But enough has been said to indicate the methodological bias of this discussion, and like any such preference it will now have to be vindicated by results.

There are some general features of Marx's usage which strike one right away. In the first place it may be remarked that the use of the bare substantive 'ideology' on its own is quite rare, and where it does occur it has none of the hypostatized solemnity that tends to accompany it in the later literature. This feature is, of course, in keeping with the inexplicit character of his theoretical approach. What is entirely typical is the use of the noun accompanied by a qualifying epithet, such as 'republican', 'German',

'Hegelian' and 'political', or in references to, for instance, the 'ideology of the bourgeoisie', and that of 'the political economist'. Equally typical is the adjectival use in which something or other is said to have an 'ideological' character. The list of subjects includes 'expressions', 'forms', 'phrases', and 'conceptions'. We hear of 'ideological contempt', of 'ideological theory', of 'the ideological standpoint', of 'ideological reflexes and echoes', of 'ideological nonsense', of 'ideological distortion', of 'ideological method' and so on. Even more distinctive is the frequency of reference to the 'ideologists', the actual spokesmen or creators of the ideological forms. Thus, he writes of Napoleon's 'scorn of *ideologists*', of 'the Young-Hegelian ideologists', of 'the *ideological cretins* of the bourgeoisie', of 'the *ideological* representative and spokesmen' (of the petty bourgeoisie and peasantry), of 'the "ideological" classes, such as government officials, priests, lawyers, soldiers etc.' and of 'the capitalist and his ideological representative, the political economist'. For what it is worth, it may be noted that approximately half of all the references to 'ideology' and its derivatives fall into this category.

Here, again, more recent Marxist literature presents a contrast, for in influential sections of it the role of the professional ideologist gets comparatively little attention. This glance at Marx's usage discloses another dimension of the contrast. It suggests that, in line with the etymology, he thinks of the ideological essentially in connection with the 'products of consciousness'; conceptions, ideas, theories, postulates and systems, and with their 'expressions' in language; formulas, names, phrases, manifestoes and so on. It is a connection which is considerably weakened in some more recent accounts of the subject. These shifts of emphasis are of great significance and will come up for explanation later. The final point to be noted here is that our examples of usage span his intellectual career from *The Holy Family* (1844) to the *Critique of the Gotha Programme*

(1875).[4] The list suggests, and this would be borne out in a complete survey, that the tone and character of the references to ideology are remarkably homogeneous throughout the period. The treatment of this theme offers little support to claims of dramatic breaks in development, but rather seems to testify to a sustained unity of thought and purpose. Hence if a precise pattern can be detected there is no reason to fear that it will not encompass the field as a whole.

Marx's interest in the ideological displays, it may be said, a high degree of consistency. The point may be more usefully put by noting that the ·issue tends to crop up regularly in his writings in a certain determinate context. This may be characterized roughly, but adequately for immediate purposes, as the context of class struggle. Thus, the ideologists are represented as the 'men of talent' of classes, the interpreters and champions of their class position. The discussion of particular ideologies, such as the 'German' and 'republican' varieties, is set firmly against a background of patterns of class dominance and sub-ordination. The ideological standpoint mentioned in the *Grundrisse* is clearly one which is fixed by the dynamic of antagonistic class relationships. It would be possible to go through the references one by one to establish that when Marx invokes the notion the dimension of class conflict is never far from his thoughts. Nor would any large effort of inference or interpretation be needed to show this: for the most part one could rely on direct textual evidence from the immediate setting of the reference. This kind of consistency is wholly in line with what was said earlier about the quality of his judgment of particular cases. Still, a programme which involved taking each one separately in turn might be unnecessarily tedious. The desired conclusion may be reached more easily by looking at what is usually taken to be a classic text and one, moreover, which rises to a rare, though still modest, level of explicitness on the concept of ideology. In the 'Preface' to *A Contribution to the Critique of Political Economy* Marx speaks of the conflict between material forces and the relations of production, a conflict which the logic of his system enjoins us to see as manifesting itself through class struggle, and goes on to refer to the 'legal, political, religious, artistic or philosophic—in short, ideological forms in which men become conscious of this conflict and fight it out'.[5] The ideological forms constitute, it seems, the medium of the class struggle in the realm of ideas. This is an important thesis, and so far, at least, the classic status of the 'Preface' can hardly be disputed. It is difficult however to progress much further on the strength of its treatment of ideology, which has all the capacity to deceive of the other elements in that seemingly transparent text. The use of 'ideological' as shorthand for 'legal, political, religious, etc.' may suggest that what is ideological is essentially to be located at a fairly high level of theoretical refinement. The reference to men becoming conscious of the conflict and fighting it out in the ideological forms may suggest that ideology is largely a matter of deliberate polemics informed by awareness of social realities. These implications, if taken seriously, would greatly restrict the scope of the concept, and are impossible to square with Marx's standard use of it elsewhere. The examples already listed help to show how little attention he pays to such constraints in practice. But it may be useful here to look in more detail at a particular text.

In the analysis of *The Class Struggles in France* the concept of ideology has an important role, and one which is unquestionably, as it were 'eponymously', fixed within the context of class struggle. It is, however, seen as operating there at many different levels of mediation, by no means all of them rarefied. In this connection may be cited the comments on the 'ideologically distinterested names' which the privileged interests had to bear in the ministries of Louis Philippe, as compared with the bourgeois republic's use of 'the bourgeois proper names of the dominant class interests'.[6] It is an example which, as well as being representative so far as its theoretical weight is concerned, seems to point with particular clarity towards the forces that shape Marx's concern with the ideological. This suggestion will be taken up later. What should be remarked now is how far the text is from depicting ideology as an instrument for attaining consciousness of the nature of the social conflict. The insurrection of June, 1848, is described as 'the first great battle . . . between the two classes that split modern society':

> It was a fight for the preservation or annihilation of the *bourgeois* order. The veil that shrouded the republic was torn asunder.

Nevertheless, Marx adds:

> The official representatives of French democracy were steeped in republican ideology to such an extent that it was only some weeks later that they began to have an inkling of the significance of the June fight.[7]

So far from men becoming aware of the nature of the conflict through ideology, it is explicitly presented here as a barrier to such awareness. It has a capacity to obscure the true significance of events which is entirely in keeping with the role assigned to it elsewhere by Marx. In *The Class Struggles in France* ideology is clearly seen as operating in a variety of guises at different levels of consciousness, and as carrying out its historical tasks more or less independently of the state of awareness of individuals or groups. Thus, the text embodies a sense of the complexity of its workings which was to be greatly developed by later Marxists, forming, for instance, a characteristic theme in the work of Gramsci. For the roots of this development in Marx it is to the concrete discussions of contemporary history that one must look, not to the schematic formulations of the 1859 'Preface'. Their lapidary effect is achieved precisely through the smoothing out of complexity. This is an element that it is important to preserve in sharpening our account of the relationship between ideology and class struggle.

It may be best if a sharper version is put forward right away, in a summary fashion, and then developed and defended in the course of the discussion. It may be introduced by noting that the context of class struggle shapes Marx's conception of ideology in a peculiarly direct way. The factor of significance in that struggle occupies the centre of his field of interest and operates there in an imperialistic style that leaves little room for other sorts of consideration. It is upon this factor that the decision to invoke the notion seems to depend in practice. The issue may be made clearer by considering a central sort of case, the classification of ideas, beliefs and theories as being 'ideological'. What one is entitled to assert on the basis of his procedure is that when he is dealing with forms of consciousness that have a distinctive role to play in the class struggle he is, in general, content to regard them as having ideological significance on that ground alone. Where he is not concerned with this aspect, or where it is irrelevant, it seems generally not to occur to him to raise the question of the ideological at all. This is to suggest that the tendency of his thought is towards making utility in the class struggle the necessary and sufficient condition for consciousness to be ideological. The defining characteristic of ideological consciousness, one might say, is its tendentiousness in this dimension. The point may be put in terms of a notion whose use in this connection has just been noted, and which is in any case a familiar one in Marx, that of 'class interests'. To say that forms of consciousness have a role in the class struggle is to say that they serve the interests of some class or other. Now the general definition implicit in Marx's practice is that forms of consciousness are ideological if, and only if, they serve class interests. To say this is to make a claim with far-reaching implications which have to be carefully worked out.

As a first step the thesis needs to be further clarified. Marx offers little direct help in trying to give a more extended account, though his practice is, as always, a source of indirect guidance and a control on results. Moreover, it provides grounds for at least one general comment. This is that the serving of class interests cannot be a matter of the causal consequences of holding or advocating certain beliefs. Their ideological status cannot depend on what interests are, as a matter of fact, served by their dissemination. Such a view easily leads to absurdity. It would be irrelevant in this connection if, as is sometimes claimed, the publication of *Capital* actually benefited the bourgeoisie, by drawing its attention to the need for some social engineering. Neither can it be a psychological question of what people are persuaded by in practice. Even if it were true, as is also sometimes said, that the effect of some contemporary 'Marxist' theorizing is to alienate the audience's sympathies from Marx and his ideas, this literature could not be assigned to bourgeois ideology on that ground alone. There may be no need to labour the point. Nevertheless, the error of inferring ideological status from causal efficacy is one to which, in its subtler forms, Marxists and others sometimes fall victim. It is a tendency quite foreign to the spirit of his own work. He is fully alive to the tricks that history plays, to the fact that, as Gramsci puts it, 'reality produces a wealth of the most bizarre combinations'.[8] Yet he does not generally feel the need to engage in empirical study of such combinations in order to be satisfied that certain ideas belong, say, to bourgeois ideology. This is, one seems entitled to say, a status they enjoy through their being the sort of ideas they are, through some essential, not merely contingent, feature. There must, it seems, be some kind of intelligible inner connection between forms of consciousness and the class interests they serve, and the existence of such a connection is what underlies the non-empirical aspects of Marx's analysis. The tendentiousness of ideological beliefs lies, one might conclude, in their capacity for 'internally' or 'logically' serving class interests.

This formula is itself, however, by no means perspicuous. It may be well to ask what can be said in a general way to tease it out, and compare the results with the evidence of Marx's practice. An obvious step is to suggest that the dimension of *value* should now be introduced formally into the story. It seems to have the correct, indeed the only possible, logical shape for the task in hand. The function of values, it may be said, is to reach out from the side of consciousness and bridge just the kind of gap with the world we are concerned with here: the existence of this conceptual space is what makes them possible and necessary. The question that then arises is what precisely is to be the role of values in explaining how ideology serves class interests. A simple answer would be that ideological complexes operate by directly incorporating evaluative elements: these are, as it were, the semantic carriers of their class tendency. Thus, they will embody an assessment or grading of, evince a *pro* or *contra* attitude towards, states of affairs and human activities; towards, that is, particular patterns of social arrangements and the practices that seek to modify, preserve, strengthen, undermine or transform them. For the interests of classes consist in these states of affairs and in the practices that have them as their objects and raw material: such items are what give the idea substance. The way in which the intelligible inner link is forged may now be a little clearer. The claim is that ideological beliefs serve class interests just by being evaluative of elements constitutive of those interests. This seems to leave one with a straight-forward enough view of how ideology works. It may be tested and, if all goes well, fleshed out by considering some examples of Marx's practice of ideological analysis.

These have to be seen in the light of what has already been noted as the peculiarly concrete and practical character of his interests. Taking the point further it may be said that what tends to dominate all else is a polemical concern with the deficiencies of bourgeois thought: the driving impulse is a desire to unmask the ruling ideas. It is entirely typical that, in realizing it, little notice is taken of the general category of 'bourgeois ideology' which has loomed so large in later discussions. Marx's attention is directed rather to the specific forms it takes in the society of his time. Among these, two particularly well-documented cases are the 'German' or 'Hegelian' ideology on the one hand, and the ideology of the political economist on the other.

The first volume of *The German Ideology* is subtitled 'Critique of Modern German Philosophy according to its representatives Feuerbach, Bruno Bauer and Stirner'. At the heart of Marx's critique of this Young-Hegelian school is a charge of failure to break radically enough with the thought of the master. The whole body of its inquiries, he asserts, 'has actually sprung from the soil of a definite philosophical system, that of Hegel', and this dependence is the reason 'why not one of these modern critics has even attempted a comprehensive criticism of the Hegelian system'.[9] Their dependence finds its most characteristic expression in a continued reliance on an idealist ontology:

> The Young Hegelians are in agreement with the Old Hegelians in their belief in the rule of religion, of concepts, of a universal principle in the existing world. Only, the one party attacks this dominion as usurpation, while the other extols it as legitimate.[10]

The radicalism of the Young Hegelians takes the form of a programme for revolt against the rule of the concepts of their elders, a revolution of consciousness . . . but a revolution confined to the realm of ideas serves, by implication, to consecrate the existing order of reality, and so their radical pretensions are in Marx's eyes a sham:

> This demand to change consciousness amounts to a demand to interpret reality in another way, i.e., to recognise it by means of another interpretation. The Young-Hegelian ideologists, in spite of their allegedly 'world-shattering' statements, are the staunchest conservatives.[11]

At best their position leads, as with Max Stirner, only to the recognition that 'I, the actual man, do not have to change actuality, which I can only change together with others, but have to change myself in myself'.[12] Here, as elsewhere in the work, there are echoes of the 'Theses on Feuerbach', written at the same time and as part of the same programme, and much of the argument may be seen as a detailed working out of the case adumbrated there against the philosophers who have merely interpreted the world in different ways instead of changing it. Essentially what these thinkers neglect or misconstrue is the significance of 'praxis', that 'real', 'sensuous', 'objective' mode of activity which consists precisely in setting out with others to change actuality. Hence it is that the rebellion proclaimed so eloquently by Stirner means in the end 'anything you like, except action'.[13]

The intellectual tone and provenance of the world of the political economist may seem remote from the tradition of German idealist philosophy. Yet from the standpoint of ideological analysis there are some striking parallels. In discussing these 'ideological representatives' of the bourgeoisie Marx returns again and again to a fundamental point, trenchantly put in *The Poverty of Philosophy*. It concerns their assumption that 'present-day relations—the relations of bourgeois production—are natural'. They are 'the relations in which wealth is created and productive forces developed in conformity with the laws of nature', and therefore are themselves 'natural laws independent of the influence of time', 'eternal laws which must always govern society'. 'Thus', he concludes, 'there has been history, but there is no longer any'.[14] If bourgeois relations of production are indeed the natural, ahistorical, quintessentially human, social arrangements, then, of course, the praxis that seeks to abolish them goes against nature and is doomed to fail. Hence, it appears that the evaluative thrust of these two examples of ideology at work is strangely similar. In each it is directed towards the denigration of praxis, the undermining of the assumption that human beings can influence the course of history by conscious, co-operative action. Taking the two together we may be said to have a diagnosis of one classic strategy of bourgeois ideology. In the course of time Marx's attention came to be directed increasingly towards the critique of political economy rather than that of idealist philosophy, and this no doubt reflects a general process of development. But here as elsewhere the question of ideology serves to enforce a recognition of deeper continuities, for while the object of the analysis may change, its controlling assumptions and methods remain the same. It may be noted, also, that the examples clearly exhibit his feeling for what is of enduring significance in the capitalist social formation. At any rate their basic insight has been taken up in a number of contemporary analyses of the workings of bourgeois ideology. It is reflected in the thesis that its most characteristic form is technical rationalism, a belief in the omnipotence of technology and a cult of its high priest, the expert. Here too the ideological process works through the assumption that what happens in society depends on forces over which ordinary people can have no control. The natural outcome of such a belief is a kind of fatalism that serves to protect the existing structure of power and wealth.

The discussion of the case-studies has now to be set in the context of the general argument. It has been claimed that, for Marx, ideological forms of consciousness are distinguished by their tendentiousness in the class struggle and that this process of internally serving class interests has to be explained through the mediation of values. The suggestion was made that ideological complexes may be thought of as serving class interests by virtue of containing evaluations of the factors that constitute them. This seems now to be fully borne out by the evidence of his practice. There is no difficulty in identifying the evaluative element in the examples. The ideology of the political economist uses such unmistakably value-laden terms as 'natural' and 'reasonable' to characterise bourgeois social arrangements. The Young-Hegelian position, for its part, is frankly prescriptive: its message is 'Let us revolt against this rule of concepts.'[15] In each case there is clearly implied an unfavourable evaluation of the prospects for a praxis rooted in material conditions and aimed at transforming the existing social order. Thus, the examples fit the proposed pattern admirably, and we seem to be confirmed in our view of how ideology works. Their significance is however not yet exhausted. It has been suggested that Marx's analysis may be taken as laying bare a classic strategy of bourgeois thought and, hence, as having a permanent significance under the conditions of capitalist society. At this point some qualifications have to be entered to avoid a serious risk of misconceiving the status of his insights.

The risk is connected with a weakness endemic in the exegetical literature. Marx's reticence has left a standing temptation to go for the premature synthesis, the delineation of the category on the strength of a few promising instances. It is important to keep a sense of the real diversity of the material so as to avoid becoming fixated in this way. Hence, one has to be careful not to read too much theoretical significance into the major examples of bourgeois ideology. If one simply bears in mind the substantial differences between them it should at least weaken the urge to insist on the paradigmatic value of either. It is sometimes suggested by commentators over-impressed with the Young-Hegelian case, that all ideology, or all ruling class ideology, necessarily has an abstract, idealist character. Thus, it may be supposed that such a class is naturally driven to divert attention from the material forces at work in society. It must tend to exaggerate the role of ideas so as to encourage the passive contemplation of their interrelations, or the belief that by changing them one changes reality. This suggestion may well have value in explaining the enduring relevance of certain ideological forms. But as a generalization about how ideology works in all societies it is entirely gratuitous, and, in its trans-historical pretensions, quite foreign to the spirit of Marx's approach. As an alleged conceptual truth it can only serve as a strait-jacket into which the phenomena are fitted at the cost of much distortion. A definition in idealist terms will not readily accommodate the case of classical English political economy. Moreover, it is out of keeping with the specific tendency of Marx's thought on various occasions. Thus, for instance, the discussion in *The Holy Family* might reasonably be taken to show an awareness of the ideological significance of a version of materialism for sections of the bourgeoisie in eighteenth-century France.[16] More generally, an insistence on the necessarily idealist character of all ideology will severely restrict the explanatory role of the concept. It seems, for instance, to rule out its use in an analysis of Stalinism, where this might otherwise be thought to have considerable value. The definition could only be made to fit such cases if its key terms are robbed of all their specificity; while if this is retained it can only be a device for forcing the phenomena, rather than registering their complexity.

The ideology of the political economist also puts one in touch with enduring habits of thought. It is easy enough to see how the assumption of the permanently valid character of existing arrangements might serve the interests of a ruling class by sapping the rationality of protest at its source. But to inflate this insight into a theoretical necessity would be to mimic the error of the political economists themselves, by abstracting particular situations and their needs out of the flux of history. There seems, in general, no reason why a ruling class should not function perfectly well with a radically historicist outlook, with cyclical or millenarian views of the nature of historical development. It should also be noted that the controlling assumption of political economy can hardly be attributed to the Young Hegelians. Their failing is not that they regard existing conditions as immutable. An important part of what distinguishes them from Hegel is precisely that they give no sign of assuming that history had come to a stop in their own time. Marx's objection is rather to the assumption that all that is needed to transform reality is a change of consciousness. Thus, it is not their lack of a conception of revolution but rather its idealist character that makes them in practice 'the greatest conservatives'. They do, after all, attack as usurpation what the Old Hegelians extol as legitimate, and the difference is worth insisting on in some contexts.

Even in political economy this controlling assumption is, in its pure form, only compatible with a good conscience under certain historical conditions. These are associated by Marx with the period in which the bourgeoisie is still a rising class and its struggle with the proletariat is as yet undeveloped. In an 'Afterword' to the first volume of *Capital* he discusses the 'bourgeois horizon' of political economy, within which 'the capitalist regime is looked upon as the absolutely final form of social production, instead of as a passing historical phase of its evolution'.[17] In its classical period, he argues, political economy is able to function within this horizon while retaining a scientific character. Later, when the bourgeoisie has conquered political power and the class struggle intensifies, it has to abandon the air of neutrality and is forced down into the arena:

> It was thenceforth no longer a question, whether this theorem or that was true, but whether it was useful to capital or harmful, expedient or inexpedient, politically dangerous or not. In place of disinterested inquirers, there were hired prize-fighters; in place of genuine scientific research, the bad conscience and the evil intent of apologetic.[18]

This marks a significant change in the mode of operation of bourgeois ideology, and it reinforces the suggestion that the case-studies embody a pattern that does not obtain universally. To note it is to be reminded of the peculiarly indirect and inferential kind of way in which their results are achieved. On the face of it the arguments are valid against all forms of praxis, against the historical significance of human agency in general. Their censure would seem to fall equally on the organized political activity of the bourgeoisie, on conservative or reactionary attempts to influence the shape of social reality. Of course the overall logic of the position is on the side of the possessing classes, of those who stand to benefit most from inertia. Nevertheless, the strategy demands a degree of boldness or insensibility which may well only be possible for a class still on the ascendant, confident of its historical role and having as yet felt no significant pressure from below. These conditions were met for the bourgeoisie, in England in the period of its classical political economy and in Germany at the time of *The German Ideology*. When they cease to obtain, bourgeois ideology loses its scientific and metaphysical detachment and comes to grips directly with the challenge of proletarian praxis. Hegelian philosophy does not remain forever the chief ideological resource of the bourgeoisie in Germany, any more than does Ricardian political economy in England.

There are other ways of bringing out the limited significance of the examples of bourgeois ideology considered so far. It is not just that their roots lie in a specific historical situation, but that their scope and content simply fail to exhaust the field of reference of a class ideology. They deal with issues that are admittedly of central importance, general views of the nature of human history and of the conditions of the production of wealth. But in themselves these cannot supply ways of conceptualizing all aspects of the field at a satisfactory level of detail. They need to be supplemented, for instance, when it comes to the question of how ordinary political phenomena are to be understood and evaluated. Here is the province of 'political ideology' as such, and in it the issues raised by proletarian praxis cannot so readily be disposed of on general theoretical grounds. The adoption of the standpoint of political ideology seems in itself to involve recognition of a *prima facie* case for allowing such phenomena a genuine importance in the world. In this sphere at least, the fact of organized political activity by the proletariat presses on the bourgeois ideologist with some urgency and calls for direct treatment. Here also, Marx's sense of what is truly significant in capitalist society leads to themes of lasting interest.

An article in the *Neue Rheinische Zeitung* discusses the question, to be taken up later in *The Class Struggles in France,* of the light shed by the insurrection of June, 1848 on the class contradictions in French society. Marx is concerned with it in relation to the attitude of the newspaper *La Réforme*:

> The *Réforme* knows no better way of changing and abolishing these contradictions than to disregard their real basis, that is, these very material conditions, and to withdraw into the hazy blue heaven of republican ideology, in other words, into the poetic February period, from which it was violently ejected by the June events. It writes 'The saddest aspect of these internal dissensions is the obliteration, the loss of the patriotic, national sentiments', i.e. of just that patriotic and national enthusiasm which enabled both classes to veil their distinct interests, their conditions of life.[19]

It is obvious that republican ideology does not rest its case upon any generalized dismissal of praxis. The tactics are rather to come to grips directly with its proletarian forms and divert them in a particular direction, from class to national issues. The underlying assumption is not that they are doomed to be ineffectual, but that they may succeed all to well in interfering with the pursuit of other goals. The appeal to 'national sentiments' is, of course, a standard resource of bourgeois thought, and one whose use was later to be greatly refined and extended. Marx is dealing with a tendency which was only to reach its full development in the next century, with Fascism at its furthest limit. Fascist ideology is, on the face of it, however, far from encouraging a quietist or contemplative attitude to events. In its emphasis on struggle, conflict, the importance of resolution and energy, and of human agency in its organized and disciplined forms, it seems at times like a parody of the Marxist-Leninist idea of praxis. The mention of it here may serve to reinforce the importance of keeping a sense of the flexibility and resourcefulness of bourgeois ideology. Indeed, the ability to do justice to those qualities is, one might suggest, the critical test for any account of ideology in the contemporary world.

It is clear that a pass cannot be achieved by pinning all hope on the ability of notions such as 'idealism' or 'fatalism' to carry the story along. But a more general conclusion also suggests itself. It is that prospects are poor for any attempt to characterize bourgeois ideology in material terms by delineating a particular content for it, or by insisting on a certain general character for its elements. To take this path is to cast one's results in an unlikely mould from the start. Where they are significant and not vacuous they seem bound to involve concentrating on a particular segment of the field and shutting one's eyes to the rest. There have been theorists who have pursued such a course resolutely, but in the end the pressure of all that is left outside is bound to tell. Marx's conception of bourgeois ideology as a collection of representations whose unity is constituted from the standpoint of bourgeois class interests is subject to no such strictures. It offers a determinate, objective criterion that all candidates have to satisfy. Yet it avoids the risk of fixation by being able to accommodate the most varied material and all the changing needs of the historical situation of the class. Thus, it has an appropriate shape for the task in hand in that it can respect the seemingly endless diversity of the phenomena while supplying their inner principle of organization.

It may advance the discussion to move at this point from issues raised by a particular class ideology to the implications for ideology in general. One way of characterizing what is distinctive in Marx's view is to say that it represents the concept in rather formal terms, in relative independence of any given content. A feeling may nevertheless persist that the ideological realm must have some more or less determinate shape about which something useful can be said. The concept can hardly be so purely formal as to be unable to resist any imputed subject-matter, and a grasp of its constitutive principle should allow some legislation as to what may come within its scope. It will be convenient to pursue this suggestion, for the moment, in relation to the model that dominates Marx's practice, the view of ideology as working through evaluations of the constituents of class interests. It seems obvious that large areas of intellectual production are bound to prove resistant to treatment along such lines. This will be true, to take a particularly important case, of the propositions and theories of the natural sciences. What needs to be said about them here seems quite straightforward. These branches of knowledge do not have the human social world as their object and must surely fail to possess the kind of evaluative significance that is in question. It is indeed hard to see how the claims of the geologist or astronomer could be internally related to class interests, as that relationship has been conceived up to now. The primary mode of interpretation that Marx gave to his thesis seems to compel a recognition of the ideological neutrality of the natural sciences. Such a consequence is, it may be said, reflected in his writings: these subjects are conspicuously absent from their various lists of the forms of ideological consciousness. The sense of a contrast or opposition between the scientific and the ideological has figured prominently, though often in a mystified form, in recent Marxist literature, and will have to be looked at with some attention later. For present purposes it is enough to note the measure of justification it can claim in Marx's work. This consists in the fact that his basic method of analysis tends to exclude the possibility that the natural sciences could have the kind of tendentiousness that is required. However, even within the guiding assumptions of that method, the situation is rather more complicated than has been suggested so far, and it is necessary to muddy the waters a little before going on to consider any wider possibilities.

The net effect of the qualifications is to warn against treating science as an undifferentiated entity to which ideology stands in abstract opposition. The first arises from the simple observation that the subject-matter of the branches of natural science exhibits varying degrees of remoteness from the concerns that define the ideological sphere, the structural antagonisms of human societies. Thus, some have more interest for the professional ideologist than others: they can more readily be drawn on for the descriptive and explanatory material that any serious attempt to render an evaluation plausible has to employ. The claims they make may be combined with straightforwardly tendentious material and incorporated within a complex that is ideological in the way depicted above. There is an obvious distinction to be drawn in this respect between those branches of science that include the consideration of man as a natural entity and those confined to the non-human world. Significantly, it is in connection with the former that questions about the ideological status of natural science tend to arise most vividly; as is shown in, for instance, the debates over the reception of the ideas of Darwin and Lysenko. These debates may serve to illustrate another kind of complication. It is connected with the possibility that scientific claims may involve covert evaluations which have ideological relevance. This may happen if, for instance, key terms in a theory have an element of the appropriate kind of force. Such terms as 'evolution', 'natural selection' or 'intelligence' may be allowed to retain, in addition to their official meaning, favourable associations from non-technical usage. The possibilities for equivocation that result may have considerable ideological significance in the right circumstances. It is a phenomenon that gets little attention in Marx's practice, with its concentration on material whose evaluative component is overt and unmistakable. The significant cases in the contemporary world are less likely to wear their hearts on their sleeves, especially in a field such as science where the professional ethos includes a commitment to ideals of 'value-freedom'. The effect of this is to ensure, if not innocence, at least that traces of guilt are well hidden. It is an important and difficult task of ideological analysis to bring such secrets to light.

At this point the course of the discussion needs to be reviewed. It has been argued that Marx's practice of inquiry through the pursuit of evaluations creates a presumption of the ideological irrelevance of the natural sciences. Admittedly, this has to be set in the light of a recognition that some branches at least lend themselves to reinforcement for ideological purposes, and that significant evaluations may be hidden in seemingly innocuous places. The effect of these concessions may be to soften the conclusion that one has to deal with sheer externality and indifference, but they do not touch its substance. It remains the case that in their typical reaches the natural sciences can have no internal connection with the defence of class interests. This is perhaps all that needs to be said. But it is possible to wonder whether such an account does justice to their true ideological potential, as suggested by, for instance, their role in the intellectual structures of late capitalism. A sense of their massive cultural significance in such societies must at least encourage one to leave the issue open a bit longer. If any further progress is to be made we shall have to retrace our line of thought to Marx's original insight, and ask whether it may not be possible to tease out its implications in some other way, to give it an alternative interpretation for practice. The insight is that ideology is the medium through which the class struggle is conducted in theory. The distinguishing feature of its forms of consciousness is that they participate in that struggle. That is to say that unless ideas have some bearing on questions of the legitimacy of the social arrangements of class society, there could be no point in labelling them 'ideological'. To depict the situation in this way is obviously to claim an indispensable role for values. But it may be that this can be conceived of along lines other than those implicit in the usual practice of Marx himself. It is at this point that his insight may be susceptible to the kind of organic development mentioned earlier. An attempt must now be made to show a possible line of such development, and the first step is to confirm that it is one that really can claim some roots in the texts.

The clearest suggestion in Marx of an alternative model for the ideological process is to be found in his treatment of religion. A convenient source is the section on 'The Fetishism of Commodities' in the first volume of *Capital*. Its main concern is to explicate the way in which, under the conditions of commodity production, 'a definite social relation between men . . . assumes, in their eyes, the fantastic form of a relation between things'.[20] In pursuing it, this suggestion is made:

> In order . . . to find an analogy, we must have recourse to the mist-enveloped regions of the religious world. In that world the productions of the human brain appear as independent beings endowed with life, and entering into relation both with one another and the human race. So it is in the world of commodities with the products of men's hands.[21]

A little further on the idea of an analogy between the religious and social worlds is sharpened by reference to particular cases:

> The religious world is but the reflex of the real world. And for a society based upon the production of commodities, in which the producers in general enter into social relations with one another by treating their products as commodities and values, whereby they reduce their individual private labour to the standard of homogeneous human labour—for such a society, Christianity with its *cultus* of abstract man, more especially in its bourgeois developments, Protestantism, Deism, etc., is the most fitting form of religion.[22]

The idea is then applied to the 'ancient social organisms of production' which 'can arise and exist only when the development of the productive power of labour has not risen beyond a low stage, and when, therefore, the social relations within the sphere of material life, between man and man, and between man and Nature, are correspondingly narrow'. 'This narrowness', it is claimed, 'is reflected in the ancient worship of Nature, and in the other elements of the popular religions.'[23] The consistent use of the terminology of 'reflexes' and 'analogies', of what 'fits' or 'corresponds', should be allowed its due weight here. Marx is pointing to the possibility that religious conceptions may mirror or duplicate the forms of the social world, with each distinctive set projecting its own image onto an other-worldly screen. The scope of such a possibility clearly extends well beyond the ideological sphere. Here, as always, one has to resist the temptation to allow the specificity of his conception, its precise identity within the theory of class struggle, to be dissolved. It must be remembered that he was prepared to speak of the ideological only in so far as the context also allows for the idea of stratification by classes. Even within the strict terms of his conception one might, of course, wish to allow ideological significance to Christianity 'in its bourgeois developments', and the mechanism of this significance needs to be accounted for. Nevertheless, our present concern is not with distinguishing what is of relevance to ideology among the varieties of religious belief. It is rather with the possibility that religion in general may provide a vital clue, perhaps even a kind of paradigm, for the understanding of an important ideological process. The model it adumbrates is one in which the effect is achieved not through issuing evaluations but through the construction of analogues. It is interesting here that Marx should wish to insist on the importance of the 'religious reflex' in connection with the 'primitive tribal community'. For the mode of analogy is often held to be characteristic of 'primitive' thought, and it is to the writings of anthropologists that one most readily turns for help in clarifying and developing the theme. A particularly rich source is provided by the work of Claude Lévi-Strauss.[24]

The issues traditionally subsumed under the heading of 'totemism' arise from the tendency to connect natural species and human groups. The problem: 'how may it be explained that social groups, or segments of society, should be distinguished from each other by the association of each with a particular natural species?' is, according to Lévi-Strauss, 'the very problem of totemism'.[25] It is necessary, he insists, to reject any attempt at functional or utilitarian solutions of it. In formulating totemic relationships 'the mind allows itself to be guided by a theoretical rather than by

a practical aim'.[26] Natural species are chosen not because
they are 'good to eat', but because they are 'good to think'.[27]
Moreover, the kind of thinking in which they are involved
exemplifies a universal pattern. It testifies to the conclusion
that 'In every one of its practical undertakings, anthropology... does no more than assert a homology of
structure between human thought in action and the human
object to which it is applied'.[28] It is to this notion of
'homology of structure' that we must now look in seeking to
develop our alternative working model for ideology.

A 'binary opposition' affords, as Lévi-Strauss remarks,
'the simplest possible example of a system',[29] and the
workings of 'a principle consisting of the union of opposites'
are allowed the largest significance in his thought.[30] This is
to be justified in virtue of a supposed natural tendency of the
human mind to operate with a logic of binary concepts: such
a logic 'of oppositions and correlations, exclusions and
inclusions, compatibilities and incompatibilities' is like 'the
least common denominator of all thought'. It is 'an original
logic, a direct expression of the structure of the mind . . . .'.[31]
The phenomenon of 'Australian dualism' offers a good
illustration of its operation in a particular case. Some
Australian societies, it appears, are divided into moieties
which function as totemic groups. This arrangement is the
basis for a dualism which, according to Lévi-Strauss, 'is
extended to the whole of nature', so that, 'theoretically at
least, all beings and phenomena are divided between the two
moieties. . .'.[32] Thus, 'the most constant characteristic' of
the moieties 'lies in their connection with totemism through
the bipartition of the universe into two categories'.[33] Such a
system reveals with particular clarity the features that
concern the present discussion. But matters are not
significantly different from this standpoint even where the
moiety division does not obtain. Thus one finds that under
the conditions of 'clan totemism' also:

> All beings, things, and natural phenomena are comprised in a
> veritable system. The structure of the universe reproduces that of
> society.[34]

The implications of all this for our theme are easy enough to draw. Lévi-Strauss explicitly represents himself as concerned with the problem of explaining how man came 'to use the diversity of species as conceptual support for social differentiation'.[35] Here is essentially the very problem of ideology too, that of explaining how theory underwrites the class structure. His answer is based on 'the postulate of a homology between *two systems of differences,* one of which occurs in nature and the other in culture'.[36] It is surely to be regarded as a primary and elemental mode of legitimation, involving as it does a spontaneous, indeed inevitable, recourse of 'savage thought': men seek real diversity in the natural order as it is 'the only objective model on which they can draw'.[37] Thus we are offered the most perspicuous image of the process we seek to explore. It is one in which the structure of the universe so reproduces that of society that wherever human beings look the forms of their culture are repeated over and over. The legitimacy of the forms, the sense of their rightness, rests on conformity to the fundamental patterns of meaning that have been discerned in experience. No larger authority could be claimed. If one had to formulate the lessons enforced by the contemplation of these structures the result would not fall naturally into the shape of an evaluation. It seems to require some such locution as: 'This is how things are'; the formula of discourse concerned with what is, rather than what should be, the case.[38] In such a manner one might hope to capture the essential conviction that the social arrangements are grounded in, and themselves exhibit, the character of reality itself. It is proper to speak of a process of legitimation in this connection, and hence to look here for a way of conceiving of the workings of ideology. It will, however, be a model that operates not 'semantically' through the incorporation of evaluative meaning but, as it were, 'syntactically' through analogies between systems. A large range of possibilities now opens up for inquiry, and there is distinguished work one can draw on to show something of them.

The issues raised by the relationship between religion and society form a major preoccupation with Max Weber. The notion of 'elective affinity' seems to promise something in common with the kind of resemblance we have been discussing and it is, according to a standard commentary, the 'decisive conception by which Weber relates ideas and interests'.[39] As this relation is our basic concern the conception may deserve a closer look. *The Protestant Ethic and the Spirit of Capitalism* sets out to investigate 'whether and at what points certain "elective affinities" between forms of religious belief and practical ethics can be worked out'.[40] As this formulation suggests, Weber's interest is in mapping connections within the realm of ideas rather than, as in the ordinary practice of ideological inquiry, with moving backwards and forwards between that realm and concrete historical situations. This fact, however, need not rob the discussion of all its relevance, and, if we are fortunate, may even serve in the end to enlarge our sense of what ideological inquiry could involve. In his attempt to work out the affinities, Calvinism and more particularly the doctrine of predestination have a special place. He argues that for ordinary believers the vital question to which the doctrine gave rise was 'How can I be sure of being among the elect?', and so the search for proofs of salvation came to be central to religious life. The answer was found in the idea of the 'calling' which implied a practical asceticism embracing all aspects of thought and behaviour. In this lies the key to the main line of affinity. The ideal of the rational organization of religious life in pursuit of signs of grace is paralleled by the ideal of the rational organization of economic life in pursuit of profit, and this latter is taken to be the hallmark of the spirit of capitalism.[41] Thus, the affinity is carried by an element that is 'formal' in the sense of implying no particular restriction on the content of the ideas it connects. This is the conception of the systematic disposition of all the details of a process in the light of a supreme goal. The reliance on such formal links is the common element of 'elective affinities' and 'homologies of structure'. The significant difference between them from the standpoint of the present discussion is that Weber is not offering a device for constituting the ideological status of ideas by fixing their social correlates, but one for connecting elements within the sphere of the ideologically given. For 'the spirit of capitalism' loses little if it is rendered simply as 'bourgeois ideology'. It finds expression in the specification and prescription of the classic bourgeois way of life, sustained by the virtues of prudence, calculation and abstinence. Clearly, this mode of consciousness is ideological in the way familiar from Marx's examples: it is evaluative of practices constitutive of class interests. What Weber's discussion points to is the possibility that such an ideology may in its turn be underpinned through affinity with some more fundamental and comprehensive set of ideas. Putting its moral in another way, one may say that it shows how beliefs which seem purely spiritual, indeed eschatological, in character may achieve ideological significance through affinity with a complex of appropriate evaluations. It is obvious that many variations are possible on these themes. The two 'models' so far distinguished may be combined in other ways so as to bring fresh dimensions of thought within the ambit of the ideological. This discussion has merely tried to illustrate some of the possibilities. It does in addition serve to suggest that a full-scale study would reveal a need to rethink traditional views of the main antipathies and allegiances in the field. It is already clear that the conventional tendency to contrast Weber's treatment of the relationship between consciousness and social reality with that of Marx needs to be qualified. At least there is nothing in the account of the Protestant ethic that is incompatible with the practice of Marxist ideological analysis. On the contrary, the effect of considering the two together is to emphasize the scope and fertility of Marx's insight. It testifies to the extent to which the conception of ideology shares in the potency of his work as a source of what is 'good to think'.

This part of the argument may be concluded with a more straightforward illustration of the 'syntactic' mode from a writer consciously concerned with questions of ideology in relation to Marxist tradition. A central theme of Lucien Goldmann's *The Hidden God* is 'the link between the economic and social position of the *officiers* of the *ancien régime* and the ideology of Jansenism'. The effective reality of their position was that they were 'dependent upon an absolute monarchy which they disliked intensely, but which had no means of satisfying their demands by any reforms conceivable at that time'. It was, writes Goldmann, 'an eminently paradoxical situation—and one which, in my view, provides the infrastructure for the tragic paradox of *Phèdre* and of the *Pensées*—where they were strongly opposed to a form of government which they could not try to destroy or even to alter in any radical manner'.[42] This tragic quality finds its fullest expression in a 'dual attitude' to the world:

> . . . tragedy believes neither that the world can be changed and authentic values realised within the framework it provides nor that it can simply be left behind while man seeks refuge in the city of God. This is why tragic man cannot try to spend his wealth or fulfil his duties in the world 'well', nor pass over these duties and abandon his wealth completely. Here, as elsewhere, tragic man can find only one valid attitude: that of saying both '*Yes*' and '*No*', of being in the world but not of the world . . . .[43]

We are presented here with a relationship whose terms, general ideas and the position of a social group, are closer than in the previous example to the standard requirements of ideological inquiry. Moreover, it is clear that the primary ideological effect in this case is achieved not in virtue of the power of ideas to evaluate reality, but in virtue of their power to reflect it by repetition of formal elements. The link between the terms is 'formal' in the same sense as before: it is susceptible to an indefinite variety of concrete manifestations. It is constituted by the factor of 'paradox', a versatile device capable of yielding the sustaining principle of a system and of permeating its details. The tragic vision insists on both the 'Yes' and the 'No', and in doing so re-enacts and universalizes the dilemma of a group held fast in a social world in which it is incapable of achieving any authentic mode of action. This is perhaps a kind of limiting case for the notion of group interests. Nevertheless, it is still possible to speak of the legitimation of a predicament, one whose ineluctability is mirrored in, and guaranteed by, the nature of human experience in general, as revealed in tragic thought. Thus, once more, the universe is made to resound to the tune of the local and time-bound. Seen in this perspective, the process by which conceptual support is secured in the ideology of Jansenism does not essentially differ from that of the totemism of Lévi-Strauss' Australians. Such a conclusion is only made the more vivid if one notes the intriguing similarities at the level of substantive characteristics; in particular, the shared dualism and obsession with a logic of opposites.

The case of Jansenism should be allowed to add its weight to the lessons of the preceding discussion. Our second model works through formal analogies which will, in its significant instances, be complex enough to sustain claims of structural resemblance. It may now be suggested that these resemblances will characteristically have something of a cosmic flavour. This mode of legitimation works best where it manages to inscribe the structures of the social situation in the forms of the universe. In that way it ensures that their repetition will be inexorable enough to generate all the authority required. Religion can hardly be considered a serious contender to provide the main cosmological support of modern industrialized societies. The obvious alternative is science and so, at this point, the issue of its ideological status seems to require re-opening. Before doing so, however, some matters of an epistemological kind should, for the sake of clarity, be got out of the way. Epistemology represents one of the two major dimensions in which it is convenient to consider the development of the concept of ideology in Marxism after Marx; the other being that of general social theory. Neither line of development could be said to flow naturally from their common starting-point, and neither can be taken far without beginning to impose demands it is ill-equipped to sustain. Together they constitute a kind of smoke-screen laid down between the contemporary observer and that original position. As part of our efforts to dissipate it the demands of social theory will form the subject of the next chapter. After that the discussion will turn to the epistemological dimension, and should then be in a position to take up again the question of the relationship between ideology and science.

CHAPTER 2

THE BURDEN OF SOCIAL THEORY

AN obvious way to try to meet the needs of social theory is to conceive of ideology as a form of group consciousness. That is to see it as a form of consciousness whose distribution is distinctive of a social group and which arises in some genetically intelligible way from the common situation of its members. Ideologies may then be individuated in terms of the groups to which they belong. Conceptions of this sort are common enough in non-Marxist sociology. What distinguishes the 'Marxist' version is the assumption that, where ideology is concerned, the appropriate groups are the basic or primary ones in the social formation. Ideologies are to be identified as those forms of group consciousness whose 'subjects' or 'bearers' are social classes. At the heart of this approach is an assumption about the distinctiveness of the mode of genesis of ideology. The key to understanding is to see it as a particular kind of socially determined thought: the primary function of the concept is to collect forms of consciousness in terms of their origin. From the standpoint of Marx's position all of this may be said to constitute a kind of genetic fallacy. Its influence has, nevertheless, been both wide and deep, and will often force itself upon our attention in the course of the discussion.

To begin with, it may be well to distinguish the thesis that ideology serves class interests from the thesis that it is determined by class interests. This latter claim may be taken in a number of ways. To see it as an instance of the genetic fallacy, it has to be allowed some theoretical significance. The idea would be that this particular kind of determination is to be incorporated within the definition of ideology. It is commonplace to find such a view attributed to Marx.[1] Yet it is neither stated nor implied in his writings, and, moreover, there is nothing esoteric about the views he actually held. They find expression again and again in remarks like those in *The German Ideology* on 'the distorted form in which the sanctimonious and hypocritical ideology of the bourgeoisie voices their particular interests as universal interests'.[2] Later in the same work he speaks of 'German liberalism' as 'empty enthusiasm, the ideological reflection of *real* liberalism', and adds that its 'liberal phrases' are 'the idealistic expression of the real interests of the bourgeoisie'.[3] The talk of ideological forms 'voicing' or 'expressing' class interests may be taken as a standard formula for Marx's conception of the relationships involved here, and is, of course, entirely in line with the thesis developed in the previous chapter of this essay. The relationships are assumed to operate not in a genetic mode but in one that is expressive and functional in the way now familiar to us. The central idea is not that ideology is necessarily engendered by class interests, but that it necessarily serves as the medium in which their conflicts are articulated.

The thesis of determination by interests may be taken in another way, as a kind of empirical generalization. It would then amount to the claim that while ideological forms may be distinguished independently of their origins, still, where these are concerned, class interests must in fact be assigned the dominant role. In assessing this view it would be well to avoid a risk of confusion by moving it out of the shadow of some large-scale, substantive generalizations to which Marx is indeed committed. There is, after all, a widespread and well-founded impression that he attached considerable significance to the possibility of giving a genetic account of the varieties of social consciousness. This reflects a determination not to allow them to function as primary units of explanation, but rather to represent them as requiring in their turn to be understood by reference to more fundamental levels of the social structure. The classic source of such impressions is, once more, the 'Preface' to *A Contribution to the Critique of Political Economy*. There one learns: 'It is not the consciousness of men that determines their existence, but their social existence that determines their consciousness.'[4] This is a difficult saying and its difficulties have been widely canvassed. However, what needs to be said now should not encroach on any of the disputed territory. It is, firstly, that however the determinant is precisely to be conceived, it is clearly a complex totality of some sort, the configuration of all the forces at work in a particular field. An exclusive concern with 'interests' could only be an undialectical isolation of individual factors here. Moreover, what is said to be 'determined' is men's consciousness as such, a category that extends well beyond the scope of the ideological, however that is defined. Hence, although the formula does, no doubt, encompass ideology it tells one nothing distinctive about it. The position is similar in regard to another general thesis often extracted from the 'Preface'. This is the idea that ideology is to be assigned to a superstructure erected on a 'real foundation', 'the economic structure of society'. Clearly, the real foundation could not with any plausibility be reduced to a matter of class interests alone. Moreover, to do justice to Marx's conception of 'the whole immense superstructure' it has to be seen as including many items, such as legal and political relations, which are not simply forms of consciousness at all. Nor will all of the forms of consciousness it involves fit naturally under the rubric of ideology. As was noted earlier, the chief clue which the 'Preface' provides to the character of the ideological forms is that in them men become conscious of the social conflict and fight it out, and large areas of the superstructure of consciousness must surely lie outside the scope of this conception. Thus, the 'Preface' does indeed encourage the view that ideology is susceptible to a genetic explanation of a particular kind, but this is a fate it shares with non-ideological forms of consciousness and with much else besides. Nothing is revealed there about the specific conditions of its production.

The discussion does, however, suggest that in trying to understand those conditions it might be well to look beyond the horizon of 'interests'. Such a suggestion is easy to reinforce from elsewhere in Marx's work. The tendency to inflate the notion into a universal genetic principle is one for which he had little sympathy. It is a tendency associated in *The German Ideology* with utilitarianism and specifically with Bentham, a philosopher 'whose nose had to have some interest before it would decide to smell anything'.[5] About the philistinism of the implications for theory Marx is as scathing as Kant or Nietzsche. His explanation of the 'apparent stupidity of merging all the manifold relationships of people in the *one* relation of usefulness' is that it arises 'from the fact that, in modern bourgeois society, all relations are subordinated in practice to the one abstract monetary-commercial relation'.[6] In its later stages at least, utilitarianism is seen as a crudely reductionist doctrine reflecting the grosser aspects of bourgeois society. Once the general doctrine is rejected, it becomes possible to think of the role of interests in a piecemeal way, distinguishing cases where it is significant from ones where it is not. It seems natural, for instance, to invoke such a contrast in characterizing the transition in bourgeois thought from 'disinterested inquirers' and 'genuine scientific research' to 'hired prizefighters' and 'the bad conscience and the evil intent of apologetic'.[7] Moreover, in so far as this transition does illustrate the contrast, it serves to remind one of the danger of neglecting its other pole, of underestimating the influence that class interests may exert in practice. Ideology is, after all, to be defined in relation to such interests, and although the relation is not genetic, it may well be that of all forms of consciousness it is genetically the most susceptible to their influence. Indeed, on Marx's account, this is in fact dominant in certain, admittedly degenerate, phases of bourgeois thought. Hence it may be that some contemporary theorists have reacted too far against vulgar-Marxist or Stalinist views of the mechanical derivation of ideology from interests. The result is a failure to give adequate recognition to the actual role such interests may play. As a corollary of this, it may be noted that an understandable distaste for conspiracy theories has sometimes left too little room for the role of conscious calculation in the genesis of ideological forms. But clearly such forms may be created and sustained through the co-operative and co-ordinated efforts of those whom Marx calls the 'active, conceptive ideologists'. Here, as elsewhere, a great merit of his approach is that it does not obscure the perception of simple truths.

These issues may be taken a little further in connection with the treatment of his predecessors in political economy. There is a fairly straightforward sense in which class interests may be said to have had a determining influence on the theories of Malthus. He is, as depicted by Marx, consciously led by the desire to promote such interests. Thus, he 'only draws such conclusions . . . as will be "agreeable" (useful) to the aristocracy against the bourgeoisie and to both *against* the proletariat'.[8] In doing so he 'seeks to *accommodate* science to a viewpoint which is derived not from science itself (however erroneous it may be) but from *outside, from alien, external interests*',[9] and to this end he '*falsifies* his scientific conclusions'.[10] Ricardo, on the other hand, is consistently presented as one of the 'disinterested inquirers' who are motivated by factors internal to the scientific enterprise, love of truth and desire to extend the boundaries of knowledge. There is frequent acknowledgement of the 'scientific honesty' which will not permit him to trim to any alien considerations. Nevertheless, it is also clear that Marx is fully alive to the ideological significance of Ricardo's work, and any satisfactory account of the matter must be able to do justice to that awareness. He is presented over and over again as arguing 'from the standpoint of developed capitalist production',[11] and the central doctrine of the ideology of the political economist, the belief that the laws of bourgeois economics are laws of nature, is explicitly attributed to him.[12] The crucial fact, which Marx does not fail to point out amid all the tributes, is simply that, regardless of questions of motivation, 'Ricardo's conception is, on the whole, in the interests of the *industrial bourgeoisie . . . .*'.[13] It is this fact that determines, in the way our argument makes clear, its significance for ideological inquiry. Thus, the difference between the ways in which class interests impinge on the formation of the thought of Ricardo and of Malthus is not reflected in any comparable difference at the level of ideological status: the fact that the one contributes to bourgeois ideology and the other primarily to that of the aristocracy is not significant here. This case may therefore be taken as reinforcing the view that such status is independent of the genetic role of interests.

It also poses problems for other versions of the genetic thesis. Thus, for instance, there is another level of determination which it might be tempting to invoke. It consists in the factor of class situation in general, 'the whole conditions of life of a particular class', and of the formative influence of class membership on the consciousness of individuals. This is a wider notion than mere 'interests'. It encompasses all the forces that impinge on the class, the complete perspective that unfolds from its location in the process of production. As such it represents a genuine dialectical totality. Yet it is not so comprehensive as to be simply identical with the 'real foundation' of society, the economic structure as a whole. It is a factor which, as we shall see, does function for Marx as an important determinant where forms of social consciousness are concerned. The point to insist on here is that it is not through the category of ideology that its influence is conceptualized. So far as his practice of ideological analysis is concerned, the formation of consciousness by class situation has no special theoretical significance. Thus, considerations of class origins do not determine the ideological status of ideas. Furthermore, there is no requirement that ideologists should be members of the class whose interests they serve. Malthus, 'the parson', was not himself an aristocrat, and 'hired prizefighters' are in the nature of the case available to the highest bidder. These are, of course, merely instances of the general truth that ideology is to be understood through its mode of efficacy and not its mode of genesis. It should also now be evident that Marx is not committed to any particular substantive thesis as to how in fact its various manifestations arise.

Ideology is, it appears, an unpromising subject for genetic inquiry in that the unity of the forms is not constituted from a standpoint that would make it theoretically fruitful. Nevertheless, the habit of genetic thinking has been strong in this area. It has frequently been assumed that causal or quasi-causal explanations are peculiarly appropriate to it. Such an assumption has tended to have a debilitating effect on ideological inquiry. In vulgar-Marxist versions it encourages the view that its central task is to trace ideas to their roots in the social background and, thereby, both to explain them and to dispose of their power, to explain them away. In the study of culture this easily leads to a philistine reductionism that altogether fails to do justice to the kind of autonomy and complexity that the phenomena possess. Marx's standard procedure, as exemplified in the treatment of utilitarianism and of classical political economy, offers no encouragement to such a tendency. In it the genetic explanation of the ideas is dialectically interwoven with the process of bringing to bear on their contents the full resources of science and logic. It is important not to sacrifice any of the elements that contribute to the richness of this strategy.

Once the habit of thinking genetically is broken, the conception of ideology as a form of group consciousness loses its main support. There is no longer any rational basis for attempts to correlate ideologies and classes on a one-to-one basis. Such attempts seem in any case bound to fail when confronted with reality's wealth of the bizarre. Marx's conception enables one to appreciate this spectacle without an intellectual surrender to it, without losing sight of the principle of unity of the phenomena. Thus, there are correlations to be established between the distribution of ideological beliefs and class membership. Bourgeois ideology may well have a tighter grip on the bourgeoisie than on other classes. But there can be no guarantee in advance of this, and in important areas one may suspect that it will not be so. The ideological force of beliefs may actually be enhanced where they rest lightly on the class whose interests they serve: such inner freedom may confer greater ease in their exploitation. Religious beliefs provide the standard illustration here. The combination of ruling-class scepticism and the piety of the subjected is familiar from many periods. In the contemporary world it is bourgeois ideology which provides the greatest difficulty for any naïvely sociological approach. Success in accommodating all its fantastic shapes must surely result in a loss of the determinacy needed to saddle the results on a single bearer. If, on the other hand, the data are tailored neatly enough to achieve this with some plausibility, it can only be at the cost of more or less arbitrary limitations of content. From the standpoint of Marx's position all such attempts are quite misconceived. Ideologies are not the sort of things that can in any significant sense be said to have 'bearers'. No doubt in every case there will be empirically discoverable groups of subscribers to the beliefs that constitute them. But, as will by now be clear from this discussion, their identity is not to be secured by reference to the existence of such groups, and nothing of theoretical importance turns on their discovery.

This point may be developed by putting the lesson of the discussion in another way. It is that to follow Marx in dealing with the ideological it is not enough to insist on the vital significance of classes. The context within which it has to be located is specifically that of class struggle, a field of force constituted by a network of antagonistic relationships. It cannot be adequately delineated by atttempts to establish connections with classes as entities conceived of in abstraction and in isolation from one another. The use of the concept in intellectual inquiry, as classically demonstrated in his work on French history, is to theorize certain aspects of the dynamic processes that make up the class struggle. The controlling impulse behind the tendencies we have been considering is to abstract the concept from this specific context and employ it on the terrain of general social analysis. This can only be done at the cost of a break with Marx's conception. It is a price which non-Marxist sociology has always been perfectly willing to pay. The problems that concern us here arise when the break goes unnoticed by Marxists or when attempts are made to reap the benefits without acknowledging that it has taken place at all. The possibilities of confusion and self-deception are then endless. An attempt will be made later to explain why it was that ideology came to embark on its general sociological career. For the present we must turn to consider an issue that now presses with some urgency, that of its relationship with class consciousness. The denial that ideology is a form of group consciousness raises it in an acute way, for on one interpretation class consciousness is itself just such a form.

A background may be supplied here by recalling some commonplaces concerning Marx's treatment of the question of social class. The first is that there is no full-scale, systematic discussion of it in his writings: the manuscript of *Capital* breaks off at what appears to be the critical point. Equally familiar is the idea that in his scattered remarks on the subject there are two distinct tendencies to be discerned. On the one hand, class is conceived of in terms of an 'objective' criterion, the location of groups in the process of production. On the other, he sometimes introduces a 'subjective' factor by requiring a certain level of consciousness for any such group to constitute a class. This duality is not the result of simple blindness or confusion. He is well aware of its existence and sometimes marks it with terminological devices, as when he contrasts a class 'as against capital' with a class 'for itself'.[14] Elsewhere, he adopts the convention of different points of view: considered in one way certain individuals form a class, while considered in another they do not.[15] It may be understandable that he feels no great need to say what is the real meaning of the term, but such tolerance of ambiguity has proved a source of difficulty for his successors. In particular, the lack of a satisfactory body of theory at this level has bequeathed an unstable basis for the discussion of the nature of class consciousness. Moreover, the discussion has naturally tended to reflect the tensions of the legacy that is available. For those who emphasize the 'subjective' criterion it becomes essential to designate the level of consciousness that is in part constitutive of class existence. A great deal of significance may then be attached to the differences between this 'true class consciousness' and the actual state of consciousness of groups defined by their relation to the mode of production. The concern with 'objective' aspects, on the other hand, encourages a different spirit in the handling of the issues. There is less theoretical pressure to mark off strict boundaries within a hierarchy of forms of consciousness. The 'spontaneous' consciousness of the members of the class is less likely to be devalued by contrast with what is higher or more authentic. Amid these complexities the characteristic preoccupation of classical Marxism has been to contest every tendency to lose sight of the distinction between class consciousness as such and the merely empirical. This is so at least in the case of such thinkers as Lenin and Lukács, and their versions of the distinction need to be considered in some detail.

The argument of *What is to be Done?* revolves around a contrast between 'the consciousness of the working masses' and their 'genuine class-consciousness'.[16] The former arises spontaneously from the historical experience of the workers and finds political expression in the trade-union struggle.

The latter, which Lenin identifies with socialist consciousness, involves an awareness on their part of 'the
irreconcilable antagonism of their interests to the whole of
the modern political and social system';[17] that is, a grasp of
the nature of the class struggle. Such a consciousness is not
to be achieved spontaneously, but only as the result of
theoretical work, and in fact is in the first instance brought to
the workers from outside, from its source among intel-
lectuals of bourgeois backgrounds. Within this framework
the term 'ideology' is used simply to denote the intellectual
armoury by means of which the class struggle is conducted.
The ideological status of ideas depends solely on the nature
of the interests they serve and is quite independent of their
origins or distribution, the intentions of their sponsors and
all other considerations. Their serving of interests is a matter
of the forms of praxis they license or enjoin. Hence arises the
insistence that '*all* worship of the spontaneity of the
working-class movement . . . means . . . a *strengthening
of the influence of bourgeois ideology upon the workers*'.[18]
The point is later restated in the clearest terms: 'the
spontaneous development of the working-class movement
leads to its subordination to bourgeois ideology . . . for the
spontaneous working class movement is trade-
unionism . . .'.[19] Socialist ideology, it appears, arises outside the range of the spontaneous consciousness of the
workers, and trade- unionism, which arises within it, is to be
accounted among the ideological resources of the
bourgeoisie: Lenin speaks explicitly of 'the bourgeois
(trade-union) ideology'.[20] It is evident from all this that for
him ideology is not in any sense a mode or aspect of group
consciousness, and the moral that classes are the
beneficiaries of ideology, not its bearers, could scarcely be
more clearly drawn. It is also clear that so far from distorting
or abandoning Marx's conception of ideology, as has often
been claimed,[21] he has penetrated right to the heart of it and
given an exemplary instance of its application. It is true that
What is to be Done? offers a highly polarized view of the

political situation. The battle lines are tightly and comprehensively drawn: 'the *only* choice is — either bourgeois or socialist ideology',[22] and 'to belittle the socialist ideology *in any way, to turn aside from it in the slightest degree* means to strengthen bourgeois ideology'.[23] But Lenin's use of the concept of ideology is logically tied to his perception of class interests, and in *What is to be Done?* the interests of the workers consist in the early overthrow of the existing system and in that alone. Everything that detracts or diverts attention from the task serves the interests of the bourgeoisie. It is perfectly possible for Marxists who perceive the reality of class interests differently to differ correspondingly in their application of the concept of ideology. Some might, for instance, be less ruthless in assigning trade-unionism to the bourgeois side. This need not signal a theoretical disagreement, but rather a different assessment of the state of the conflict in a particular historical situation.

In *History and Class Consciousness* the distinction we are exploring is introduced in the following way:

> By relating consciousness to the whole of society it becomes possible to infer the thoughts and feelings which men would have in a particular situation if they were *able* to assess both it and the interests arising from it in their impact on immediate action and on the whole structure of society. That is to say, it would be possible to infer the thoughts and feelings appropriate to their objective situation.

Given this possibility, it emerges that 'class consciousness consists in fact of the appropriate and rational reactions "imputed" (*zugerechnet*) to a particular, typical position in the process of production'. 'This analysis', it is added, 'establishes right from the start the distance that separates class consciousness from the empirically given, and from the psychologically describable and explicable ideas which men form about their situation in life.'[24] In an essay written many years later, and used as a preface to the English edition of

History and Class Consciousness, Lukács was to assert that
by the notion of an 'imputed' class consciousness he 'meant
the same thing as Lenin in *What is to be Done*? when he
maintained that socialist class consciousness would differ
from the spontaneously emerging trade-union consciousness in that it would be implanted in the workers "from
outside" . . .' .[25] This claim is hard to accept just as it
stands. Obviously, Lenin's distinction is only applicable to
the proletariat, while Lukács's works, in principle at least,
for all classes. But even in the case of the proletariat the two
sets of terms do not precisely coincide. Its empirically given
consciousness will not always be identical with trade-
unionism, a form characteristic of a relatively advanced,
though still pre-revolutionary, stage of development.
Moreover, since the imputation of authentic consciousness
is not simply that of the consciousness which a class ought
ideally to have, but is limited by the objective possibilities of
the historical situation,[26] what is imputed to the proletariat
will not always amount to a socialist consciousness. This too
is only appropriate at a certain stage of development. It
appears that the one distinction could at best only be thought
of as a special case of the other, its expression in the
conditions of mature capitalism. Nevertheless, when the
necessary qualifications are made, Lukács is right to claim a
connection. The common factor is the determination to
establish and maintain the significance of the gap between
true class consciousness and the spontaneous or empirically
given. It is, moreover, a determination which has deep roots
in the tradition to which both writers belong. It arises
naturally, as we have seen, from the general logic of Marx's
treatment of class and class consciousness. There are also
quite direct and specific links that may be traced. As an
epigraph to the essay on 'Class Consciousness' Lukács uses
a well-known passage from *The Holy Family*:

> The question is not what goal is *envisaged* for the time being by
> this or that member of the proletariat, or even by the proletariat as a

whole. The question is *what is the proletariat* and what course of action will it be forced historically to take in conformity with its own *nature*.[27]

In the original, Marx had gone on to claim that 'a large part of the English and French proletariat is already *conscious* of its historic task and is constantly working to develop that consciousness into complete clarity'.[28] Thus, he distinguishes between the ideas that some or all members of the proletariat happen to have at any moment and the consciousness appropriate to the historical role of the class. Clearly, we are at this point in touch with an important and enduring theme in the classical Marxist tradition. There seem to be no good grounds for impugning the orthodoxy of Lukács's contribution to it.[29]

On the face of it, the view of ideology presented in *History and Class Consciousness* fits with equal ease into the pattern set by Marx and Lenin. Its credentials are easy enough to establish. Ideology is consistently placed in the context of 'the central fact of capitalist society: the class struggle'.[30] The references to it are suffused with the appropriate kind of imagery: one reads of 'ideological weapons', of 'ideological self-defence', of 'ideological leadership', of 'ideological champions', of 'ideological crisis', of ideological defeat', of 'ideological capitulation' and of the 'social conflict reflected in an ideological struggle for consciousness'.[31] The impression left by such unity of tone is clear and striking. Lukács, like Marx, is prepared to invoke the notion of ideology only in connection with the class struggle, and, given this, requires no further conditions to be met. Such a conclusion is borne out by the treatment of his own theoretical position. Historical materialism is described as 'the ideology of the embattled proletariat',[32] and Marxism as 'the ideological expression of the proletariat in its efforts to liberate itself'.[33] Evidently he is prepared to regard any set of ideas as ideological, provided only that it has a role in the primary social conflict. Thus we find ourselves in the same conceptual universe as in the discussion of Marx and Lenin. The elements are, of course, handled in a distinctive way, but this need not raise any doubts about the larger identity. A tradition in this respect embracing Marx, Lenin and Lukács might now be thought to be firmly established. It must, however, be acknowledged that such a conclusion would be hard to square with some recent influential criticisms of Lukács. These are worth considering in detail, and not merely in order to make our conclusion secure. They are important because of the standpoint from which they are delivered: this lies at the heart of the most significant tendencies in contemporary Marxist accounts of ideology.

The case brought by Nicos Poulantzas revolves around the charge that Lukács has an 'historicist' view of ideology. What this amounts to in detail may, by now, have a familiar ring. In the historicist picture ideologies appear as 'number-plates carried on the backs of class-subjects'. Each ideology is presumed to stand in a genetic relationship to a class and its character is entirely determined by that relationship. In this conception 'there can be no *world over and beyond* the ideology of each class', and so the 'various ideologies each function as it were in a vacuum'. Poulantzas's main objection is that the conception is unable to account for, or even acknowledge, the complexity of the patterns of dominance and subordination in any actual society. On such a view, 'it would be impossible (i) to establish the existence within the dominant ideology of elements belonging to the ideologies of classes other than the politically dominant class and (ii) *to account for the permanent possibility of contamination of working class ideology by the dominant and petty-bourgeois ideologies*'. Indeed, it makes it 'impossible to see the effects of ideological domination by the dominant ideology on working-class ideology'.[34]

Poulantzas's critique moves at a rarefied level, untroubled by any specific references to Lukács's writings. What is essentially the same case has been developed in a less magisterial way by Gareth Stedman Jones in writing on the Marxism of the early Lukács'.[35] There the points made by Poulantzas are repeated and developed in a number of ways. Once again the emphasis is on 'the drastic and crippling simplification' which Lukács's view of ideology imposes. In order to fit in with it 'historical development is pared down to a simple procession of economic-ideological totalities expressing the life conditions of successive class-subjects'. 'The necessary complexity of any given social formation' is, Stedman Jones affirms, 'annulled from the outset by this imaginary parade'.[36] The Lukácsian view of the genesis of ideologies comes under specific attack: 'For Lukács, the dominant ideology in a social formation will be a pure manifestation of the ideology of the dominant class, and the ideology of the dominant class will be a pure reflection of the life conditions and conception of the world of that class.' Such a view is thought by Stedman Jones to be entirely mistaken, and he quotes Poulantzas to drive the conclusion home: 'the dominant ideology does not simply reflect the life conditions of the dominant class-subject "pure and simple", but the political relationship in a social formation between the dominant and dominated classes'.[37] In the case of the dominated classes, he continues, 'Lukács's model leads to even more serious results'. For there is 'no room in it for conceiving the possibility of a dominated class which does not possess a consciousness which is neither "ascribed", nor that of the ruling class, but is *uneven* and *impure*'. The truth, however, is that 'history is littered with examples of this impurity in which radical proletarian class instinct is often deeply overlaid by bourgeois ideological veneers of different sorts, or in which genuine proletarian ideology is mixed with contaminations from allied, rather than enemy classes— peasants or urban petty producers, for example'. Stedman Jones cites some fairly familiar historical examples to show what he has in mind, and concludes that 'Lukács condemns all this to silence.'[38]

A convenient starting point for assessing the Poulantzas-Stedman Jones critique is provided by the question of 'ideological contamination' and, in particular, its implications for the dominated classes. The complaint against Lukács is that he is unable to see these effects or has to condemn them to silence. Such blindness and deafness are, it is supposed, the natural outcome of his basic assumptions. Hence, the study of these symptoms should throw some light on the organic source of the disease.

A first reaction might well be to conclude that the allegations are entirely groundless. For Lukács is fully alive to the significance of phenomena which it would be natural to subsume under 'ideological contamination' and which are so treated by his critics. He refers to these phenomena explicitly and with the utmost seriousness on many occasions. He is, that is to say, much occupied by the contaminating influence of bourgeois ideology on the proletariat. His admiration for Rosa Luxemburg derives in part from her campaign for 'its ideological emancipation from its spiritual bondage under opportunism'.[39] He warns of the danger that it might 'adapt itself ideologically to conform to . . . the emptiest and most decadent forms of bourgeois culture'.[40] He speaks of the power of non-proletarian ideologies '*within* the proletariat itself',[41] and insists that 'the mere fact of victory does not free the proletariat from contamination by capitalist and nationalist ideologies'.[42] Such references are far from representing an enforced recognition of facts that cannot be theoretically assimilated. On the contrary, ideological contamination of this kind has a vital place in the intellectual scheme of *History and Class Consciousness*. A basic assumption running throughout the work is that: 'As the product of capitalism the proletariat must necessarily be subject to the modes of existence of its creator.'[43] Yet the prospects of the revolution depend on its success in shaking off this inheritance. For 'the proletariat has been entrusted by history with the task of *transforming society consciously*'.[44]

Its revolution is uniquely 'the revolution of consciousness': the achievement of true class consciousness is the precondition for fulfilling its historical role. To put the point in terms of the distinction with which we began: the outcome of the final battle 'depends on closing the gap between the psychological consciousness and the imputed one'.[45] Hence arises that 'terrible *internal ideological crisis*' of the proletariat to which reference is made again and again.[46] The process of closing the gap, and so overcoming the crisis, is precisely one of sloughing off ideological impurities, of eliminating the traces of contamination by alien ideologies. The largest issues, the fate of the revolution and with it that of humanity in general, depend on its successful completion. It seems fair to conclude that not only is Lukács able to acknowledge and theorize the phenomenon of ideological contamination, but it has in truth a central place in his view of the historical process. Indeed, it would scarcely be an exaggeration to say that, from one point of view, *History and Class Consciousness* is a treatise on the nature and significance of such contamination and on the means by which it is overcome.

Some part at least of the case against Lukács has now evaporated. It will not do to say that he cannot conceive of the possibility of a dominated class whose consciousness is uneven and impure. For him this seems rather to be the normal condition of the proletariat in bourgeois society. It may be, however, that recognition of this does not suffice to dispose of the anti-historicist critique. For that contains a number of elements it does not clearly distinguish. At times it appears that Poulantzas and Stedman Jones interpret 'ideological contamination' in another way. They are concerned rather with the situation in which a class ideology might be said to be 'impure' in that it derives from heterogeneous sources. The trouble with Lukács would then be his mono-factorial view of the genesis of ideologies, their springing into existence as pure reflections of the historical situation of isolated classes. The charge is not that he cannot recognize the effect on psychological consciousness of alien ideologies, but that he cannot recognize the effect on an ideology of elements that arise outside the 'life conditions' of its class, from outside the range of the determinants of its spontaneous consciousness. Understood in this way, 'ideological contamination' turns out to be a sort of converse of the phenomenon discussed previously. The first comment to be made about it is that Lukács, quite clearly, holds no such simple-minded view of the genesis of ideologies as a general thesis. He is no more committed than is Marx to any such view. Historical materialism is, after all, 'the ideology of the embattled proletariat' and Lukács is as aware as anyone that it was originally brought to the proletariat 'from outside'. But Poulantzas and Stedman Jones do not seem inclined to press the general charge here. Their interest is rather in the treatment of the dominant class and it is in this light that their objections deserve to be considered.

When this is done, however, the charge of failure to cope with complexity seems to have as little substance as in the previous interpretation. As Lukács depicts the state of ruling-class ideology at the time of writing *History and Class Consciousness*, heterogeneity of source material is virtually its dominant characteristic. For the bourgeoisie is also suffering an 'ideological crisis',[47] precipitated in its case not by the decisive stage in the struggle for imputed consciousness, but rather by the fact that the 'ideological leadership' is slipping from its hands.[48] It has become unable 'to defend itself ideologically from its own resources',[49] and, as a result, has made an 'ideological capitulation to historical materialism'.[50] This process is presented in terms that echo Marx as a descent from intellectually respectable positions to 'a more or less conscious attempt at forgery'.[51] In the final phase, 'the objective disintegration of capitalist society is reflected in the total incoherence and irreconcilability of opinions joined together in one ideology'.[52] This is perhaps a kind of limiting case, an ideology at the end of its tether. Nevertheless, the fact that Lukács can envisage it as the culmination of a gradual process suggests that he suffers from no theoretical block here. That is, he finds no difficulty in accepting that elements in the ideology of the dominant class may be derived from outside the 'way of life' of that class. Such he believed to be the actual condition of bourgeois ideology in his own time.

It appears that whether complexity is understood in terms of unevenness of empirical consciousness or of eclecticism of ideological content, Lukács is well able to accommodate it within the terms of his theory. This is hardly a surprising conclusion. The views attributed to him amount, after all, to a remarkable naïve and mechanical sort of schematism. Even a slight acquaintance with the power and subtlety of his thought should make one sceptical of this, and no very deep reading of *History and Class Consciousness* is needed to confirm such scepticism. Indeed the question that now arises is how it is that Poulantzas and Stedman Jones come to advance with such assurance a set of criticisms that pass so very wide of their target. Some special explanation seems called for here. It will hardly do just to put it down to personal defects of vision: the failure involved is on too grand a scale. It looks more like a case of the kind of theoretical blindness they attribute to Lukács. Thus, it is tempting to suggest that they themselves may be captives of a picture that obscures what would otherwise be obvious. When one looks more closely, the outlines of just such a picture begin to emerge and its significance goes well beyond the present occasion. For it underlies a great deal of contemporary thinking about ideology, and serves to cut such thinking off from the views of Marx, Lenin and Lukács. As such it is the source of a serious dislocation within Marxism and merits our full attention.

It may be helpful at this point to note a curious feature of the way in which Poulantzas and Stedman Jones refer to the question of contamination. This suggests yet another perspective on what they have in mind. Poulantzas writes, as we have seen, of the contamination of working class ideology by the ideologies of other classes and of its domination by such ideologies. Stedman Jones writes in the same connection of the 'contamination of a pristine class ideological essence by elements derived from the ideologies of other classes'.[53] All of this differs in a significant way from what one finds in Lukács. As the references already given suggest, his characteristic concern is with the contamination of the psychological consciousness of a class by the ideology of another class, rather than with anything that might be conceived of as the mutual contamination of ideologies or ideological essences. To note this helps to make the objections of Poulantzas and Stedman Jones more intelligible. It may be that a part at least of what they include in 'ideological contamination' is indeed condemned to silence by Lukács: his premises rule out in advance the possibility of any recognition of it. For if one assumes that ideologies serve class interests and that the interests of classes are irreconcilably opposed, there is a difficulty in seeing how there can be any contaminated, in the sense of 'compound' or 'syncretic', ideologies. It becomes impossible for class ideologies to incorporate significant elements from the ideology of other classes without losing their identity. For that depends on the master they serve and they cannot serve two at once. In this sense ideologies for Lukács do, necessarily, have a certain pristine purity. But in this he is fully in line with the requirements of Marx's original conception. It is worth noting here that Lenin also does not speak of the contamination of one ideology by another. Rather he speaks, as we have seen, in a way fully consonant with Lukács, of 'the strengthening of bourgeois ideology upon the workers', of 'the subordination of the working class movement to bourgeois ideology' and so on.[54] Moreover, he insists that to turn aside from the socialist ideology in the slightest degree is to strengthen bourgeois ideology. Clearly there is no room for 'impure' ideologies, in the sense being considered, within Lenin's scheme: its nature ensures that all impurities are displaced outside. Moreover, the ideology of the proletariat is, for him, to be identified with the theory of socialism. It is not clear what could be meant by the intellectual domination of this theory by bourgeois ideology. It could scarcely admit of such domination without ceasing to be a genuinely socialist theory devoted to the interests of the working class; without, that is, ceasing to constitute proletarian ideology. Of course, it is conceivable that it might suffer defeat in the ideological struggle and even lose all practical efficacy in the world, but that is another matter: what is ruled out is the peace of an ideological compromise. Such a conclusion is dictated by the character of Marx's conception and, in particular, by the criteria of identity it lays down for ideologies. Thus, the difference between speaking of ideologies contaminating each other, and speaking simply of them as contaminating classes or class movements is a significant one. The latter usage is in keeping with the logic of Marx's position in a way that the former is not. The fact that this is employed so unselfconsciously by Poulantzas and Stedman Jones suggests that they have failed to grasp or to assimilate that logic.

The nature of the failure needs to be specified more precisely. As a first approximation, it should be linked with the empiricist perspective which dominates their approach. Such a perspective is implicit in the way they refer to the issue of contamination. It is as if ideology were a universal, liable to be instantiated with varying degrees of purity, and, in any particular case, one can test for this, as with beer or water. The same tendency emerges more strikingly else-where. It does so, for instance, in the use made by Poulantzas of a contrast between the 'spontaneous ideology' of the working class and its 'revolutionary ideology'.[55] Such a distinction could have no place in Lenin's or Lukác's world. For them, revolutionary ideology simply *is* the ideology of the working class, and the phrase 'spontaneous ideology' could only be a mask for its ideological sub-ordination to the bourgeoisie. The use of the contrast reinforces the suggestion that for Poulantzas ideology is essentially an 'empirical' concept. That is, its nature is such that the question of whether the criteria governing its use have been satisfied in any particular case is one that calls for empirical observation. For Marx, Lenin and Lukács its nature is by contrast specifically 'theoretical' in that the use of the criteria involves operations on ideas, a species of theoretical analysis. It is hard to see how the presence and character of a 'spontaneous ideology' could be determined except through a connection with the spontaneous, empirically-given consciousness of a class. The criteria to be applied are of a sociological kind. The influence of this 'sociologism' is also discernable in the general character of the case against Lukács. The central thrust of it is that he is unable to cope with the actual complexity of the data: his view of ideology is found to be lacking in explanatory value when applied in the analysis of social formations. But such a criticism rests on a misconception of what he is trying to achieve. The point at issue here deserves to be taken a little further.

An important theme in the critique of Lukács is that he misconceives the role of ideology as an instrument of cohesion, as, in Gramsci's metaphor, a kind of social 'cement'.[56] In his work, 'the role assigned to ideology through the medium of the class-subject is that of the principle of totalizing a social formation'.[57] Poulantzas accepts, and indeed wishes to stress, that ideology 'has the particular function of *cohesion*'.[58] This is not, however, to be conceived of in a Lukácsian manner: 'its specific, real role as unifier is not that of constituting the unity of a formation (as the historicist conception would have it) but that of reflecting that unity by *reconstituting* it on an imaginary plane'.[59] It is hard to escape the feeling that something has gone radically wrong with the argument at this point. For Lukács, as indeed for Marx, ideology has no special role to play in a theory of what it is that holds social formations together. This is, no doubt, a legitimate subject of inquiry, but it is not one in which either of them was particularly interested. If there is a position on it to be extracted from their work, it will have no special link with their conception of ideology. That, as we have seen, has its peculiar sphere of activity in the theory of class struggle, and is ill-fitted to constitute the main pillar of a general theory of social cohesion. The problem seems to be that Poulantzas is so much the prisoner of his own theoretical preoccupations that he assumes they must be central for others also. Hence, Lukács is awarded poor marks in a competition in which he is not entered and about whose results he might not greatly care. The fact that so perceptive a commentator can fall so easily into such assumptions about his subject is itself of some general significance. It signals one of those occasions in intellectual history when a massive subterranean shift has gone unnoticed by the toilers on the surface. Thus it points to precisely that hidden chasm in the Marxist tradition which we are concerned to explore.

For the present, however, we must remain with Lukács in order to tie some loose threads together. It is now clear that depending on how ideological contamination is understood it is either fully catered for within his theory, or is excluded as a matter of principle. In either case the criticism of him on that score fails of its purpose. Its failure should make one look again at his alleged 'historicism', the presumed source of all the difficulties. The discussion so far has shown that it must, at any rate, be an historicism which is compatible with an acute sense of the complexity of the historical process. It is one which does not need to rely on a conception of classes as pure subjects operating in a vacuum, or of ideologies as essences distilled under such clinically-sterile conditions. It must also be an historicism which operates without a doctrine of the inevitability of the goal towards which history is moving. Lukács's position on this is not entirely unequivocal, and there are phrases which, taken out of context, might be used to support a hard line. But the most characteristic and consistent theme is that only the downfall of capitalism is inevitable through its internal contradictions.

Whether it is succeeded by socialism or by 'the destruction of all civilization and a new barbarism' depends on the free action of the proletariat. The course of historical development opens up the 'objective possibility' of a successful revolution, but it offers no guarantee of the outcome.[60] It is at this point, however, that one comes upon what is really the central weakness of the intellectual structure of *History and Class Consciousness*. From the standpoint of internal coherence, at least, the trouble, one might say, is that the work is not nearly historicist enough. There is a gap in the argument which a throughgoing historicism might have been able to bridge. It arises from the lack of a rational connection between the analysis of capitalist society and the vision of the future, from a failure to theorize adequately the historical transformation represented by the proletarian revolution. Even a doctrine of economic determinism of the kind associated with the Marxism of the Second International might have been able to avoid the incoherence here, whatever its weakness in other respects. But, of course, no such solution was available to Lukács. His revolution is a revolution of consciousness, conceived of in terms which are in some respects reminiscent of the radical Young Hegelians of the previous century. He is, however, a Hegelian who has assimilated what he takes to be the central point of the 'great polemic against Hegel in *The Holy Family*', that consciousness has to be conceived of as immanent in history.[61] It follows that he has no room for any equivalent of the 'World Spirit'. This, for him, is a transcendent demiurge which in Hegel's scheme is the real subject of history behind the shadow-play of the spirits of the individual nations.[62] But now the historical process has lost the source of its teleological energy, and the 'ruse of reason' is no longer available to work its magic. At the time of *History and Class Consciousness* he had nothing substantial to put in the place of these devices. The result, to use an expression he favours himself, is an *hiatus irrationalis* in thought, the absence of any theoretical foundation for his hopes of the socialist society. He came to realize this of course, and it forms the core of the later self-criticism. In the essay used as a preface to the new English edition he diagnosed a failure to grasp the centrality of the category of human labour and thus to arrive at an adequate conception of praxis.[63] The young Lukács is a thinker in a process of transition, unable to enjoy the benefits either of the position he has left behind or of the one he has not yet fully assimilated. As a Hegelian without 'the ruse of reason' and a Leninist without an adequate conception of the historical role of the party, he has nothing with which to oppose mechanistic fatalism except what he later refers to as 'voluntaristic ideological counter-weights'.[64] It is this kind of irrationalist voluntarism that constitutes the fatal defect of *History and Class Consciousness*. It is a defect much more adequately captured under the label he later proposed himself of 'messianic utopianism',[65] than through any talk of 'historicism'. Indeed, leaving aside the points of coincidence, the self-criticism is generally to be preferred for accuracy and penetration to the critique we have been discussing.

The hiatus in *History and Class Consciousness* has, as one might expect, its consequences for the treatment of ideology. The main one is simply that the significance of ideological factors is consistently overrated. The central role of the 'ideological crisis' reflects this estimate. At times it seems as though the class struggle itself is nothing but the struggle to overcome the crisis; a battle in, and for, consciousness. 'This reform of consciousness', we are told, 'is the revolutionary process itself.'[66] Such an emphasis may readily be seen as an aspect of the idealism that haunts the work. But it does not in itself amount to a conceptual disagreement with Marx and Lenin, where the specific issue of ideology is concerned. Indeed, so far as this goes, Lukács's idealism may not have been altogether a handicap in the circumstances of the time. At least it protected him from the temptation to cash in the concept in empiricist terms and from the sociologism that was to overtake the Marxist tradition. It left him suitably placed to respect the distinctive status which it has as a 'theoretical' concept in Marx and Lenin. The particular significance of his work, it may be suggested, lies in the way it develops the possibilities latent in this position right up to, and sometimes beyond, their natural limits.

At this stage accounts have still to be finally settled with his 'historicism'. For it must now be admitted that the accusation can feed off elements that are genuinely present in his thought. At the risk of over-simplification, one might say that its plausibility largely derives from generalizing what he says about the agency of the proletariat in history to all other classes. The proletariat is indeed an historical subject in a special sense. It is 'the identical subject-object' which resolves 'the antinomies of bourgeois thought', and thereby fulfils the programme of classical German philosophy. This is a vast and incongruous metaphysical burden, and the thesis fully merits the later strictures on it as 'an attempt to out-Hegel Hegel'.[67] Nevertheless, even here it is worth insisting that Lukács has mythologised a theme which in itself is a legitimate, indeed inescapable, part of the tradition of classical Marxism; that of the unique historical role of the proletariat. In reacting against the form in which he casts it, one must be careful not to forget the substance. This point may be illustrated with reference to the specific question of consciousness.

A persistent emphasis is laid in Lukács's text on the 'unique function of consciousness in the class struggle of the proletariat'.[68] This uniqueness consists in part, as we have seen, in the fact that for the proletariat alone true class consciousness is the necessary precondition of historically effective action. Hence, ideology, the indispensable instrument of such action, must in this case enjoy a distinctively close relationship with class consciousness. The ideology of the proletariat, one might say, can only truly exist as the expression of its class consciousness. Indeed, Lukács specifically equates 'ideological maturity' and the attainment of such consciousness, where the proletariat is concerned.[69] Here all opportunism and electicism has to vanish. It was not always so in history, and the contrast is sharply drawn:

> Whereas in the class struggles of the past the most varied ideologies, religious, moral and other forms of false consciousness' were decisive, in the case of the class struggle of the proletariat, the war for the liberation of the last oppressed class, the revelation of the unvarnished truth became both a war-cry and the most potent weapon.[70]

This sense of the special relationship between the class consciousness and the ideology of the proletariat is also to be found in Lenin. The true class consciousness of the proletariat is socialist consciousness, and its ideology is the theory of socialism. Everything that falls short of this signifies and perpetuates the domination of the bourgeoisie. Thus, in the work of both writers one finds the vision of a unified structure of consciousness centred on the proletariat. In this vision all duality is overcome: the breach between the spontaneous and the authentic, the empirical and the rational, is healed; and ideology, the intellectual armoury of the class, is a pure expression of the resulting unity.

The ultimate source of this vision is, of course, Marx himself. The belief expressed in *The Holy Family* that the English and French proletariats had begun to achieve their true historical consciousness has already been noted. An optimism about the possibilities of proletarian consciousness was to remain a familiar and enduring strand in his thought. We are in contact here with a phenomenon which is central to the classical Marxist picture of social development. Many important details are treated in different ways by the theorists we have been considering. They differ in particular over the nature of the process through which the vision is to be realized, and those differences might loom large in other contexts. For present purposes it is more important to stress what they have in common. This is the image of a structure incorporating ideology and class consciousness whose elements are organically integrated and whose realization is intimately bound up with the role of the proletariat in history. In this central image lies the solution to many puzzles. As yet, however, it lacks some essential ingredients and we must wait on a later stage of the discussion to supply them.

It is time to take up again the question of the positive use to which Poulantzas wishes to put the concept of ideology in the general theory of social formations. This is, as we have seen, to conceptualize an apparently universal need. The function of ideology is to provide the cohesion which every society requires to survive and perpetuate itself. At the start of his discussion of these matters Poulantzas refers the reader to a work by Louis Althusser.[71] It is a hint which it might be well to take up at once. The way in which Poulantzas develops the theme is heavily indebted to Althusser, down to the details of its verbal formulation. To say this is to say nothing particularly contentious, nothing that Poulantzas would be likely to dispute. Hence, it may prove more rewarding to pursue it in connection with Althusser's own work. There it finds a richer development than is feasible in a study to which it is not wholly central. Moreover, the great influence exerted by his views on ideology, not least in Britain,[72] entitles them to consideration on their own account. In the present case the need is reinforced by the fact that they offer some important clues to the nature of that dislocation in Marxist thought which is among our chief concerns.

In the passage referred to above Poulantzas is drawing on what are perhaps the most distinctive and significant themes in Althusser's treatment of ideology. They are also those which have attracted the main bulk of critical attention. Nevertheless, they are not the only ones it contains. The problem recurs again and again in his work, and is sometimes characterized in ways difficult to integrate with the theses

extracted by Poulantzas. This is especially so where the
focus of interest is on ideology not as a social reality but as a
mode of cognition which needs above all to be distinguished
from science. Moreover, the material used by Poulantzas is
derived from the period of what one must now call the
'earlier Althusser'. For present purposes the main texts of
the period are the essays in *For Marx*, the contributions to
Reading Capital and the essay on 'Ideology and Ideological
State Apparatuses'. A significant break is represented by
the work published in English as *Essays in Self-Criticism*.[73]
Taken together, the two phases constitute a pattern of great
interest for our inquiry. It is convenient to start with the
earlier one in order to grasp the whole. This body of work
has something of the same interest as that of the young
Lukács in that it encapsulates certain tendencies in the
treatment of ideology taken to their furthest limit. As such it
has a kind of exemplary significance in charting the
possibilities afforded by a tradition.

The first step is to consider the ways in which ideology as a
form of apprehension is characterized in the earlier
Althusser. One suggestion is that it is distinguished by
ignorance of its own 'problematic'; that is, the intellectual
framework within which its problems arise. Althusser
remarks that it is 'the way the problems are posed which
constitutes the ultimate ideological essence of an ideology',
and adds that:

> An ideology (in the strict Marxist sense of the term—the sense in
> which Marxism is not itself an ideology) can be regarded as
> characterized in this particular respect by the fact that *its own
> problematic is not conscious of itself.*

Thus, for Marx, an ideology is 'unconscious of its
"theoretical presuppositions", that is, the active but
unavowed problematic which fixes for it the meaning and
movement of *its problems* and thereby of their solutions'.[74]
A second, and perhaps more characteristic, suggestion of
the same general type is that the essential character of
ideology consists in the way it prejudges the solutions of its

problems from the start, while science is genuinely open and allows for the indefinite expansion of knowledge. This is a point which 'defines the essentials of ideology, in its ideological form, and which in principle reduces ideological knowledge . . . to a phenomenon of *recognition*'. Hence it is that:

> In the theoretical mode of production of ideology (which is utterly different from the theoretical mode of production of science in this respect), the formulation of a *problem* is merely the theoretical expression of the conditions which allow a *solution* already produced outside the process of knowledge because imposed by extra-theoretical instances and exigencies (by religious, ethical, political or other 'interests') *to recognise itself* in an artificial problem manufactured to serve it both as a theoretical mirror and as a practical justification.[75]

In opposition to all this, Althusser stresses the need to leave the '*necessarily closed*' space of ideology 'in order to open a new space on a different site—the space required for a *correct posing of the problem, one which does not prejudge the solution*'.[76]

Considered as attempts to delineate two radically different cognitive modes, these remarks can hardly be regarded as particularly successful. Awkward cases spring all too readily to mind. Throughout Althusser's writings he tends to accept the natural sciences as genuine sciences, and is generally content to maintain that Marxism is scientific in more or less the same sort of way. Yet on widely-held views of the nature of these subjects they have not been significantly marked by selfconsciousness about pre-suppositions. Indeed, on some accounts it would seem to be almost a distinguishing feature of science that good work in it can be produced by people with little insight in this respect. Moreover, a widespread desire to achieve clarity there may be a symptom of crisis rather than normality.[77] With ideology, on the other hand, such clarity may be directly functional, at least in those important cases where it is a deliberate apologetic. Thus, it may be the professional ideologist rather than the scientist who benefits most from transparency of assumptions. It is true, of course, that the ideologist's vision is necessarily restricted by the horizons of the historical situation, but this holds for the scientist also. Whatever superior insight is ascribed to him, it will have to respect such structural limitations. It is now not at all clear how such an ascription could provide the basis for the kind of distinction that Althusser requires.

Neither does it seem helpful to present the distinction as one between forms of inquiry which prejudge their results and those which do not. On the familiar conception of mathematics as a postulate system it would thereby qualify as the paradigm of an ideology, a conclusion that would not be welcome to Althusser. Moreover, something is prejudged in all inquiry; at least in the sense that it will operate with assumptions that impose some constraints on what could count as a solution to problems. This much seems to be implied in the notion of a 'problematic'. But it will be just as true of scientific inquiry as of any other kind. Hence, if the prejudging requirement is stated in general terms it will fail to do any work at all. If, however, it is tightened up, so that it is a question of prejudging at some level of detail, the distinction that results may fail to carry any conviction. For much that seems undeniably ideological is bound to escape. Successful ideologies will be resourceful and loose-jointed enough not to have to prejudge all particulars. Their effectiveness may depend on leaving many issues genuinely open; so that, for instance, there is room for intellectual discoveries in bourgeois economics. Thus it appears that there are difficulties in Althusser's formulation which a successful version of the prejudging criterion would need to confront and overcome.

It is not easy, however, to be sure just how much weight attaches to these difficulties, and the problem is connected with the uncertain status of the original theses. They have rather the appearance of stipulations adopted to meet the needs of particular stages in an argument. But little sustained

use is made of them as such, and without the concrete details
this would provide it is hard for criticism to get a grip:
example and counter-example have, as it were, to operate in
a vacuum. All of this may not matter greatly in the present
case. For one thing, it is clear that ideology as so far
understood in Althusser has little or nothing in common with
the views of Marx. It has been assumed to be a mode of
inquiry whose methodology is defective and which needs, in
order to become scientific, to develop more sophistication in
this respect. But Marx's conception cannot be pinned down
in such a way. It has, to put it no stronger, to be understood
in relation to a practical and social dimension. The extent of
the differences may be experienced in other ways. They are
implicit from the start in Althusser's overriding concern with
the character of the distinction between ideology and
science. It is a concern which arouses no sympathetic chord
in Marx. His antipathy to the substantival idiom has already
been noted, and in the earlier Althusser this idiom is
deployed on a lavish scale. Even more significant are the
essentialist assumptions about the nature of meaning that
seem to underlie its use: it is as if 'ideology' and 'science'
were metaphysical entities whose essences have to be
extracted by the theorist and displayed in their fundamental
opposition. The influence of such assumptions is pervasive
in the earlier period and extends even to the more distinctive
and important theses on ideology to which we must now turn
our attention.

   In contrast to the ideas discussed so far, this second
position is marked by an awareness of the social dimension
of ideology. Indeed, the existence of this dimension is now
taken to constitute the contrast with science: 'ideology, as a
system of representations, is distinguished from science in
that in it the practico-social function is more important than
the theoretical function (function as knowledge)'.[78] It
would be difficult to exaggerate the scope of the claims made
for this practico-social function. Thus we read that 'ideology
is eternal',[79] that 'man is an ideological animal by nature',[80]

and that 'ideology is as such an organic part of every social totality'.[81] 'Human societies', it is said, 'secrete ideology as the very element and atmosphere indispensable to their historical respiration and life.' No attempt is made to evade the full implications of these views:

> Only an ideological world outlook could have imagined societies *without ideology* and accepted the utopian idea of a world in which ideology (not just one of its historical forms) would disappear without trace, to be replaced by *science*.

Hence, '*historical materialism cannot conceive that even a communist society could ever do without ideology . . .*'. This conclusion is then restated in the clearest terms: 'ideology is not an aberration or a contingent excrescence of History: it is a structure essential to the historical life of societies'.[82]

What, one must ask, is the theoretical basis for such assertions? If the texts of the earlier period are taken together a fairly coherent picture can be made to emerge without much pressure. The first step is to note the condition under which ideology is said to be indispensable in any society: it is so '*if men are to be formed, transformed and equipped to respond to the demands of their conditions of existence*'.[83] It performs this function through a process of 'hailing', of 'interpellating' individuals as subjects. The category of the subject is, for Althusser, 'constitutive of all ideology', and it is so in so far as '*all ideology has the function (which defines it) of "constituting" concrete individuals as subjects*'.[84] This constitution is to be understood in both senses of the key term. The individual is interpellated as 'a free subjectivity, a centre of initiatives, author of and responsible for its actions', and as 'a subjected being, who submits to a higher authority, and is therefore stripped of all freedom except that of freely accepting his submission'.[85] Through the constitution of individuals as subjects in this double sense the life of society is sustained and, in particular, the reproduction of the relations of production is guaranteed. The final matter to be settled here by way of exegesis is how precisely it is that ideology performs its task of constituting individuals as subjects. The answer is that it does so by enmeshing them in an imaginary relation which represents to them their real relation to their conditions of existence:

> In ideology the real relation is inevitably invested in the imaginary relation, a relation that *expresses* a *will* (conservative, conformist, reformist or revolutionary), a hope or a nostalgia, rather than describing a reality.[86]

For individuals, to live in ideology is to live 'in a determinate (religious, ethical, etc.) representation of the world whose imaginary distortion depends on their imaginary relation to their conditions of existence ...'.[87] For them such a fate is inescapable: it is the price that is paid to ensure the continuity of social existence.

This is a complex structure of argument and deserves to be looked at closely. A convenient way to start is by focusing on the question of why exactly it is that ideology is held to be indispensable in every society, including the classless society. It must be said at once that Althusser offers little in the way of detailed argument for the thesis. At one stage in the discussion in *For Marx*, however, there occurs what appears to be just such an argument. The suggestion is made that a purely instrumental use of ideology is impossible, so that 'a class that *uses* an ideology is its captive too'. This point, he goes on, enables one to answer the question of 'what becomes of *ideology* in a society in which classes have disappeared'. For what may now be said is this:

> If the whole social function of ideology could be summed up cynically as a myth (such as Plato's 'beautiful lies' or the techniques of modern advertising) fabricated and manipulated from the outside by the ruling class to fool those it is exploiting, then ideology would disappear with classes. But as we have seen that even in the case of a class society ideology is active on the ruling class itself and contributes to its moulding, to the modification of its attitudes to adapt it to its real conditions of existence (for example,

legal freedom)—it is clear that *ideology (as a system of mass representations) is indispensable in any society if men are to be formed, transformed and equipped to respond to the demands of their conditions of existence*.[88]

The significance in philosophy of little nuggets of argument is, no doubt, easy to exaggerate, and the value of the work of major thinkers may depend on them only to a limited extent. Nevertheless, when an example is offered it may be well to consider it carefully to see if it really does establish what it claims. In the present case one may get an impression of close argument directed to an important conclusion. A use is made of a certain logical apparatus; ('If . . . then . . . But as we have seen . . . it is clear that . . . '), and so it seems to invite formal consideration as a piece of reasoning. When viewed in this light one has to conclude that it is quite unsuccessful, in that it involves the elementary fallacy of 'denying the antecedent'. ('If ideology were just a cynical myth, then . . . But it is not. Hence . . . '). The point is worth noting here, just to counteract any impression that a connection has been established between the tendency of ruling classes to live in their own ideology and the necessity of ideology in a society without classes. This has not been done, and so far the conclusion is unsupported. Yet it does surely stand in need of some support.

The need takes an acute form in virtue of quite specific features of Althusser's position. It is not that there is anything necessarily dubious about the project of a general theory of the sources of social cohesion. Such a theory might well need to operate with the notion of some kind of universal social cement, and no great harm is done if this is designated by the label 'ideology'. The results would have little in common with the theoretical role of the concept of ideology in Marx and Lenin, but that in itself is no objection. The various attempts to give an account of the process of 'socialization' in non-Marxist sociology may perhaps be seen as contributions to such a programme and as attesting its viability. What makes Althusser's version contentious is the sustained insistence that ideology involves the distorted, imaginary relationship. The specific question to be answered is why it is that human beings are necessarily condemned to live in this opacity, to be cut off from an awareness of the real conditions of their existence. There seem to be no further detailed arguments worth examining at this point, and one might be tempted to dismiss the whole thesis as simply gratuitous or 'metaphysical'. It deserves less summary treatment, however. An attempt should be made to set it in some larger framework on which it could draw for significance and solidity, to uncover its underlying 'problematic'. One might ask what has to be assumed in order to make sense of the claim that the imaginary relationship is necessary if the requirements of society are to be met.

The answer must surely involve reference to an assumption of an inescapable measure of tension between the human individual and the social subject, a sense of the incompatibility of two sets of neeeds. Society is obliged to impose its constraints on the development of individuals, and the fulfilment of their potential would threaten the foundations of its existence. It is as if some 'old Adam' or 'noble savage' had perpetually and ruthlessly to be suppressed, and a clear view of the process on the part of its victims would be inimical to its smooth operation. Hence it is that socialization necessarily involves ideology, that complex of special measures which are our particular concern. Such a picture of society as an alien power standing over and against the individual, a source of external pressures, intent on 'forming' and 'transforming' him to its purposes has, of course, a long intellectual pedigree. At times Althusser seems aware of the possibility of embarrassment from this quarter, and takes pains to exorcise the ghosts that lurk there. Thus, for instance, there is an obvious one it might be tempting to raise with the spell: 'Men are born free, but are everywhere in ideology.' But, as if to forestall just this possibility, there is his insistence that 'an individual is always-already a subject, even before he is born'. This is so in virtue of 'the ideological ritual that surrounds the expectation of a "birth", that "happy event" ': the child is 'appointed as a subject in and by the specific familial ideological configuration in which it is "expected" once it has been conceived'.[89] It is difficult to know what to make of this. The moment of conception is not itself the occasion of an ideological ritual, and the expectations it leads to take time to gather force. Moreover, the foetus is not a subject in either of the senses Althusser has distinguished, the responsible author of actions or the subject of authority. It may be said that it is potentially both, but a potential subject is precisely not 'always-already' a subject. Perhaps, however, his remarks should not be taken in too literal a spirit. They constitute rather a little fable in which society is cast as the wicked fairy, lying in wait for the unborn with its ideological spells. It is a fable that should not be read innocently. The purpose is to disarm criticism by reducing to vanishing point the gap between the individual and the subject, to deter attempts to drive a wedge at this point in the structure of argument. But as such it is bound to fail. The gap is provided for in the theory from the start and it will not matter how far the origins of the process of fusion are pushed back. That is to say, the theoretical difference remains in spite of all attempts to secure identity of reference on each particular occasion. These attempts do nothing to allay the suspicion that one is confronted here with an odd kind of romantic individualism in Marxist trappings.

The general character of Marx's own thinking on the relationship between society and the individual presents a sharp contrast. Its spirit is fully Aristotelian: 'Man is a *zoon politikon* in the most literal sense: he is not only a social animal, but an animal that can be individualized only within society.'[90] This leaves no room for any useful distinction between the human individual and the member of society, but at most only for one between the human animal, the biological entity, on the one hand and the social individual on the other. Society is for Marx too much the unique authentic medium of human existence for a sense of the tension between individual and social to gather any universal significance. It is true that a relationship describable in those terms may be said on his view to characterize certain historical epochs, and notably that of capitalism. But the refusal to accept that it is the ineluctable human condition is central to the significance of his thought as a whole. To note this is to be jolted into an awareness of the practical implications of Althusser's view of ideology. Underlying it is the assumption that the life of reason and the demands of social existence are necessarily incompatible so far as the mass of mankind is concerned. This is not a novel insight: it is rather a perennial theme of conservative social thought. But it is difficult to reconcile with socialism in any recognizably Marxist version. The idea of the socialist society is precisely that of a state in which the two conditions are satisfied harmoniously, in which the fullest development of the individual is not merely compatible with. but is a precondition of, a truly human social existence. If this goal is, in principle, unattainable it becomes difficult to see how anyone could have good reasons for being a socialist: theory is now cut off from the springs of action.

The 'political immobilism' implicit in Althusser's position has often enough been the subject of comment.[91] Critics have not failed to note the other in-built peculiarity of its elitism. For ideology is always to be contrasted with science; and while the mass of mankind is condemned to live in the imaginary relation, the theorist has access to an alternative. The peculiar social implications of this duality are never brought into focus by Althusser himself. Nevertheless, the critics are surely right in supposing that they arise inescapably from the treatment of his central categories. Indeed, if assessed in terms of criteria of cognitive achievement, the classless society turns out to be rather less egalitarian than capitalism. For there the ruling class is, as we have seen, also the captive of ideology. In the classless society the masses remain in this condition while the theorists who have made the transition to science may be presumed to live in transparency and freedom. No extended commentary is needed to point up the distance between this vision and that of Marx.

The discussion of the views of Poulantzas and Althusser started from their rejection of the class-subject conception of ideology. This rejection is quite uncompromising so far as it goes. There remains, however, a sense in which it is not radical enough: it fails to engage with the deepest level of the problematic. There one has to speak not of a break but rather of an underlying continuity. The element of continuity arises from the failure of all these theories to identify and hold fast to the precise region in conceptual space in which the notion of ideology is anchored by Marx and Lenin. Both the Althusserian and the class-subject views allow it to slip its moorings in the theory of class struggle and drift into the vaster waters of general social theory, the region that bourgeois social thought has always claimed as its own. In a more sympathetic vein one may say that what has happened in each case is that ideology has come to be assigned new functions in theorizing the superstructure as a whole. At the level of detail these functions are conceived in different ways within the two perspectives. But the overall unity of purpose entitles one to bracket them together in contrast to the tradition that runs from Marx to Lukács. As one might expect these deep-rooted connections show themselves on the surface in a variety of ways.

Some of them may conveniently be considered in connection with the question of reification. The point involved here may be brought out by noting that each of the positions in question embodies a sort of caricature of bourgeois notions of property. The key to understanding ideology, it is assumed, is to find its owner. Poulantzas and Althusser see clearly that classes cannot possibly fit the bill. Nevertheless, they proceed as though on the assumption that the identity of ideology is only to be secured by settling it on an individual proprietor as a specific item of property. Such an approach treats the issue of its identity in a way analogous to that of a physical object, and, hence, illustrates one way in which the suspicion of reification may arise. Instead of class-subjects, however, they offer what might be called a theory of society as the subject. Ideology is a substance which human societies secrete in their innermost being as necessary to their respiration and life, and custody of it is to be assigned to the social formation as a whole. Here it is even harder than with the class-subject conception to detect a sense that behind the ideological forms stands any concrete mode of human activity at all. There is little room for the role of the professional ideologists in whom Marx was so interested, the 'wholesale manufacturers' of the ideas that fuel the class struggle. The conception of ideology as a substance perpetually emanating from the social structure belongs in a different world from that of his concern with 'real, active men' who are producers of ideas as well as material goods. From the standpoint of such a concern it can only appear as an attempt to mystify the true nature of certain human artefacts characteristic of a particular stage of history.

That stage is the epoch of class struggle, a slice of historical time which, however vast, is still not co-extensive with the whole. The function of the concept of ideology in intellectual inquiry is to theorize certain processes involving conflict and contradiction, and thus its mode of operation is specifically dialectical in character. There is a sense in which the general cast of thought of the earlier Althusser is unsympathetic to this kind of understanding. It is more at home in dealing with the solidity of elements of structure than with the fluidity of processes. Its natural bent is not so much dialectical as taxonomic. The deepest impulse, illustrated in the treatment of the science-ideology antithesis, is to get the phenomena assigned to firmly fixed and delineated categories. It is as if intellectual problems called for a species of quasi-legal decision making and the achievement of understanding consisted in establishing the appropriate rubric. This is a familiar tendency in the history of thought: it underlies the varied forms that scholasticism has taken in different periods. It is, moreover, easy to see how it encourages the reification of categories. Its standing temptation is to impose a frozen solidity that allows the work of classification to proceed in an orderly way. All of this is a long way from the radically dialectical universe of Marx, Lenin and Lukács. The conclusion seems forced that the frequent declarations in the earlier Althusser of intellectual loyalty to Marx 'express a will' rather than 'describe a reality'. Indeed it is hard to avoid giving a prominent place to the category of will in characterizing this body of work. Its distinctive mode is an unrestricted assertiveness that proceeds as if all organic links in thought could be established and sustained by sheer ambition. Part of its exemplary value is that it shows what can be achieved in this mode and its objective limitations.

The threads of this discussion may be drawn together by returning to the source of Althusser's difficulties. If his earlier treatment of ideology is considered in relation to the original Marxist conception its most striking feature is the neglect of class struggle. That factor is allowed no distinctive, strategic role in his thought.[92] In the light of this recognition one could now reconstruct the criticisms that have been outlined here. Most obviously, perhaps, it accounts for the vulnerability to doubts about the political implications of his work. Moreover, it is the loss of the secure anchorage in the theory of class struggle, and of the historical specificity it imposes, that enables him to wander onto the terrain of speculation about all conceivable forms of society. Hence it is the ultimate source of the tension between the professions of allegiance to Marx and the unprecedented burdens laid on the notion of ideology. It is also the crucial neglect that underlies the undialectical character of his thought. For class struggle is the natural home and medium of existence of the Marxist dialectic: the interpretation of capitalist society must be lacking in dialectical force if it is not placed at the centre of the stage. In this respect the class-subject and society-subject theories are alike defective. Both fail to see that the ideological context is constituted not by relationships between hypostatized categories but by the boundaries of a field of force, a network of dialectical interactions. A phrase favoured by Althusser in another connection may be helpful in characterizing this case: it is, one might say, a failure to appreciate that ideology too may be viewed as a 'process without a subject'. The insistence on finding one for it is bound to distort its significance for Marxist thought. At this point, however, one turns to the later work. For the break with his earlier self is largely constituted by the rediscovery of the factor whose absence we have been deprecating.

The primacy of class struggle is the central theme of *Essays in Self-Criticism*. Its neglect by John Lewis forms the burden of the polemic in the first part of the book, and the new definition of philosophy as 'in the last instance, class struggle in the field of theory' is invoked over and over again.[93] Moreover, the earlier writings are specifically castigated for their shortcomings in this respect. Thus, for example, in connection with *For Marx* and *Reading Capital*, Althusser writes: 'we had not yet appreciated the exceptional importance of the role of the class struggle in Marx's philosophy . . .'.[94] Moreover, he is now inclined to accept the judgment of his 'more politically-oriented' critics that 'the class struggle does not figure *in its own right*' in these works.[95] 'What was essentially lacking in my first essays', he remarks, 'was the class struggle and its effects in theory . . . '.[96] The change of heart seems complete, and its effects are beneficial in just the ways one would expect.

Clearly, he has now greatly improved his position in relation to the 'politically-oriented' critics on the Left. The change also shows itself in a different kind of concern with the dialectic, and specifically with the central category of contradiction. The connection here is explicitly made by

Althusser himself. The earlier work is stigmatized as follows: 'The absence of "contradiction" was taking its toll: the question of the class struggle in ideology did not appear.'[97] For all the significance of this development, it must nevertheless be said that there are limits to his transformation into a dialectician. For one thing, he still has misgivings about the risk of the complete dissolution of structures into processes. These find expression in, for instance, the insistence that the dialectic must be *'subjected to the primacy of materialism'*.[98] Elsewhere, he writes of Marx's care in 'submitting the dialectic to the constraints of the topography'; that is, of the base—superstructure model of society, 'the metaphor of an edifice whose upper floors rest, as the logic of an edifice would have it, on its foundation'.[99] The point of this emphasis is clear enough: it is intended to guard against 'the idealist temptations involved in the dialectic'.[100] The results, however, are not altogether satisfactory. It is not enough to counterpose to the temptations of idealism what is in effect a general warning against allowing thought to become too dialectical. What is needed is an adequate account of the specific character of the materialist dialectic which would show how it differs in its elements and mode of operation from that of the idealists. Such an account would dissolve the false antithesis implied in the slogan of the primacy of materialism. However, it will not do to judge Althusser harshly here. He makes no extravagant claims for his warnings, and indeed recognizes that they are not a substitute for a satisfactory account of the materialist dialectic.[101] The lack of such an account is the permanent scandal of Marxist philosophy in general, and he is hardly to be blamed for failing to provide one at this point. Moreover, the benefits of his shift of perspective are already substantial enough.

For the hitherto frozen categories have now begun to thaw and take on life and movement, a development he marks in a gnomic way. A footnote is provided in which he refers to the 'Marxist-Leninist thesis' that 'puts the *class struggle* in the front rank', and goes on to explain what, philosophically, that means: 'it affirms the *primacy of contradiction* over the *terms* of the contradiction'.[102] What concerns us here is the particular way in which the terms have begun to liquefy and register the play of the dialectical process. The results are most clearly seen in the rejection of the earlier view of the 'epistemological break' in Marx's development from ideology to science. He now condemns the way in which the break was conceived and defined 'in terms of an opposition between *science* (in the singular) and *ideology* (in the singular)',[103] or, as it is put elsewhere, 'in the form of the speculative distinction between *science* and *ideology*, in the singular and in general'. From this 'rationalist-speculative drama', he adds, 'the class struggle was practically absent'.[104] Later, he refers to the way in which 'every science . . . causes its own theoretical prehistory, with which it breaks, to appear as quite erroneous, false, untrue', and comments: 'there always exist philosophers who will draw edifying conclusions; who will draw out of this recurrent (retrospective) practice an idealist theory of the opposition between Truth and Error, between Knowledge and Ignorance, and even (provided that the term "ideology" is taken in a non-Marxist sense) between Science and Ideology, in general'.[105] In the light of what is said elsewhere the implication seems clear that he himself had drawn out just such an idealist theory, relying on a non-Marxist sense of 'ideology'. The distaste for attempts to develop a general contrast between 'Science' and 'Ideology' (or *science* and *ideology*) may be taken as encapsulating his reaction against the reifying tendencies of the earlier writings and brings him much closer to the spirit of Marx's treatment of these matters. In addition to all this there are remarks in the *Essays in Self-Criticism* which seem close to embodying a fully authentic Marxist conception of ideology. That is to say, the notions of class interests and class struggle are sometimes specifically invoked in connection with the ideological. Thus, for instance, there is the remark that:

'Each ruling exploiting class offers . . . "its own" explanation of history, in the form of its ideology, which is dominant, which serves its class interests, cements its unity and maintains the masses under its exploitation'.[106] There is also the suggestion that 'Marxism recognizes the existence of ideologies and judges them in terms of the role which they play in the class struggle'.[107] At this point it must be recognized that we are dealing with an overthrow of previous convictions on a substantial scale and, hence, with what is, in personal terms, a considerable achievement. The task before us is to determine its boundaries, to discover just how far Althusser has succeeded in establishing his position in a line of continuity from Marx and Lenin.

When the matter is approached from this viewpoint there are some serious reservations that have to be made. Even the apparent felicity of the phrases just quoted turns out on a closer look to be a source of disappointment. For these are not satisfactory formulations. The categorial significance of the service of class interests is not adequately recognized by simply including it in a list of social functions. Moreover, it is misleading to suggest that Marxism recognizes the existence of ideologies and, as if it were a separate operation, judges them in terms of their role in the class struggle. For Marxism is able to recognize them solely in virtue of that role. It is the core of their identity, not a source of norms for assessing what is identified independently. More generally, it may be said that what is lacking in these formulations is an appropriate sense of occasion, an awareness that anything of theoretical significance is at stake in them. They are presented in a low key as findings of Marxist sociology, not as contributions to the groundwork of a Marxist conception of ideology. This is now a rich and interesting situation. It is as if Althusser, in the course of the evolution of his thought, has been forced into contact with what is truly central in Marx's position, but is unable to come to terms adequately with the nature of its centrality. If one casts about to find the stumbling-block it will not prove necessary to look very far.

As a preliminary point it may be noted that he is far from wishing to repudiate the earlier work in its entirety. This is made clear on a number of occasions, not least in the text containing the main arguments which accompanied the submission at the University of Picardy of some of the earlier writings, including *For Marx* and the contributions to *Reading Capital*, for the degree of *doctorat d'Etat*.[108] It may help to take the discussion a stage further if one recalls another familiar objection to the view of ideology presented in those writings. This is directed to its heavy epis-temological bias,[109] shown most obviously in the persistent concern with science and ideology as higher and lower forms of cognition. The pressure of this factor has itself now eased and the result is shown in, for instance, a tendency to attach a lesser importance to epistemology in general.[110] Neverthe-less, it remains a significant influence which makes itself felt in a number of ways. Thus, it appears that so far as 'the antithesis science/ideology' is concerned, it is only in 'its *general*, rationalist-speculative form' that it must be rejected, in order that it may be ' "reworked" from another point of view'.[111] The reworking is not carried out in *Essays in Self-Criticism*, and what the alternative viewpoint would actually consist in is not entirely clear. Obviously, it would have to take account of the new status accorded to the class struggle. But it seems equally certain that it must continue to register some version of the old epistemological hierarchy.
For this has by no means been banished from the pages of the *Self-Criticism*. In their standard uses, 'ideology' and its derivatives continue to carry a weight of pejorative meaning.[112] Besides, Althusser insists that the terms 'theory' and 'science' must remain, and that this 'is neither "fetishism" nor bourgeois "reification" '.[113] Both are still to be contrasted favourably with 'ideology' where cognitive status is concerned. This emerges in, for instance, the reference to 'Lysenko's "science" ', which was no more than ideology'.[114] Writing of what he still finds valuable in the earlier work, he remarks: 'We were attempting to give back

to Marxist theory, which had been treated by dogmatism and by Marxist humanism as the first available ideology, something of its status as a theory, a revolutionary theory.'[115] Moreover, the assumption is maintained that a science develops by breaking with its ideological pre-history. Thus, with reference to the 'Three Sources' of Marxism; German philosophy, English political economy and French socialism, he insists that one must ask '*how* this ideological *conjunction* could produce a scientific *disjunction* . . . how and why, when this conjunction took place, Marxist thought was able to *leave ideology*'.[116] The answer suggested is that it is as a consequence of adopting a class theoretical position that 'Marx's treatment of his object, Political Economy, takes on a radically new character: breaking with all ideological conceptions to lay down and develop the principles of the science of History'.[117]

It seems safe to conclude that Althusser is far from breaking radically with the epistemological preoccupations of his past. There remains an important sense, even if now more diffuse and attenuated, that by contrast with science, ideology is necessarily connected with what is cognitively dubious or defective in some way. It is this hangover which prevents him from doing justice to his new sense of the central reality of Marx's position. That is, it blocks the way to a recognition that ideology is to be distinguished just in terms of its function in the class struggle and that other considerations are irrelevant to the definition. But, of course, we are dealing here with a factor that is not simply an obstacle for Althusser alone. The insistence on the epistemological connection is a pervasive feature of contemporary discussions of the Marxist conception of ideology. A detailed consideration of it can now no longer be postponed.

CHAPTER 3

THE BURDEN OF EPISTEMOLOGY

THE thesis of this essay is that the role of ideas in the class struggle constitutes the substance of Marx's conception of ideology. To say this is to imply a systematic indifference on his part to other sorts of consideration; an indifference that extends to the cognitive status of the forms of consciousness that fall within the ideological realm. For Marx, it may be said, ideology is not an epistemological category. Thus, in particular, it has no necessary connection with what is cognitively suspect or deficient in any of the ways these qualities may show themselves. It may safely be remarked that these assertions run counter to an established tradition of interpretation and comment. Examples of it have already been noted, and others will occur from time to time in the course of the discussion. It may be unnecessary, even invidious, to cite references apart from those that arise naturally in this way. The tendency in question is so prevalent that even a slight acquaintance with the literature yields a wealth of illustrations. The epistemological theme is affirmed there again and again, often as the one certain factor in an otherwise chaotic situation or as the kernel of the original doctrine untouched by later revision. It is an important part of our thesis that such claims have no basis in Marx's thought and, hence, that this body of literature is dealing in a fantasy. It is a conclusion which has now to be firmly established by developing the arguments for it in detail.

To begin with, it should be noted that there is no difficulty in citing textual evidence in its support. In the 1859 'Preface' ideology is seen as supplying the intellectual weapons of all parties to the social conflict.[1] As Marx is far from supposing that there is nothing to choose between the merits of their ideas, the implication of cognitive indifference seems clear. In *The Communist Manifesto* one learns that when the class struggle nears the decisive hour 'a portion of the bourgeoisie goes over to the proletariat, and in particular, a portion of the bourgeois ideologists, who have raised themselves to the level of comprehending theoretically the historical movement as a whole'.[2] Theoretical comprehension of the whole is, it appears, accessible to bourgeois ideologists: what is incompatible with their status is rather the decision to go over to the other side in the class struggle. All this is quite in line with what our thesis would lead one to expect. An equal significance should be attached to the sustained evidence of his practice in the writings on contemporary history. As we have seen, the concept of ideology has a strategic role in the analysis of *The Class Struggles in France*. Any attempt to read the work on the assumption that its operation there is constrained by considerations of cognitive status would, however, be doomed to fail. There is no suggestion in it that anything would be gained by correlating the views of the various groups with points on a cognitive grading chart. Such a project could have little point in the context of an attempt to cope with the myriad forms that consciousness takes in a particular, dynamic phase of class struggle. What is required for that is a categorial concept, embracing all the phenomena in question and yielding an idiom in which they may be discussed. It is precisely this requirement that is met by ideology, and its ability to meet it is the key to its role in the analysis. The ability rests on the kind of epistemic neutrality being argued for here.

The argument has, however, not yet come to grips with the chief source of the vitality of the opposing view. The assumption that ideology has an epistemological significance for Marx is all too often made with little regard to the need for evidential support. Indeed, there may be said to exist a tradition in this respect which by now has its own momentum. Nevertheless, there is a particular text which is almost invariably pressed into service when the need is felt with special urgency or when it can no longer be ignored. A misreading of *The German Ideology* lies close to the heart of the complex of assumptions we wish to challenge. There is another point which should be mentioned here. It is that even commentators who are not committed to the epistemological doctrine in a general way have sometimes believed that the links between ideology and cognitive defect are drawn with unusual tightness in that work. Such a belief may then encourage attempts to exhibit Marx's career as a succession of discrete phases or at least to emphasize the episodic character of its development. It is part of our argument that his treatment of ideology lends no support to such attempts, but rather testifies to a deep-seated continuity of thought. For these reasons it is necessary to suggest at least the outlines of a reading of *The German Ideology* that will fix it in its proper place within the general picture.

There is a contrast used by Gramsci in connection with another work by Marx that may help, if not pressed too hard, to suggest the kind of perspective that is needed. For *The German Ideology*, too, should not be viewed as primarily a 'theoretical' work but rather as 'a chapter of cultural history'.[3] The point of this emphasis is specifically to deny that it is concerned to develop a theoretical account of ideology. It offers no shortcuts to wisdom on the subject but shares in all the obliqueness and reticence one finds elsewhere. These extend in particular to the failure to provide a definition of what is presumably the key term in the analysis.[4] When we have worked one out for ourselves it turns out not to be significantly different from that implicit in the other writings. As a chapter of cultural history the work has to be set in all its concreteness against the background of the period. Its concern is not with ideology as such but with a particular variety, the *German* ideology, through its 'representatives' and 'prophets'. This ideology is grounded in a philosophical system, Hegelian idealism, with which Marx fundamentally disagrees. It is, moreover, a system which he regards as peculiarly seductive, which dominated the intellectual climate of his time and place, and from which he had only lately succeeded in freeing himself. *The German Ideology* is the settling of accounts with this 'erstwhile philosophical conscience' through the exposure of quite specific kinds of error and confusion. It is these circumstances which account for the frequency and intensity of the aspersions cast on the ideological forms discussed in the work. Such attempts to characterize particular cases are, however, not to be inflated into a full-scale, theoretical commentary.

At this point one may begin to move closer to the details of the text. Its treatment of ideas is, from the outset, firmly situated within the context of antagonistic relations between classes, and is pervaded above all by the recognition that: 'The ideas of the ruling class are in every epoch the ruling ideas'.[5] Throughout the work the reader is never allowed to forget that the thinkers are the spokesmen of classes, for the most part of the German petty bourgeoisie, and that their ideas have implications for the balance of class forces. The prospects of inserting any wedge at this point between *The German Ideology* and the later writings seem hopeless. It should also be remarked that ideology is sometimes referred to in it in ways that are strikingly difficult to reconcile with any suggestion of cognitive defect. There is, for instance, that account of how large-scale industry, through universal competition, 'destroyed as far as possible ideology, religion, morality, etc., and where it could not do this, made them into a palpable lie'.[6] This is one of the rare occasions on which the use of the unqualified substantive signals a temporary shift of attention away from the main target. Significantly, it is accompanied by an equally temporary loss of interest in castigating ideological error. Hence, it accords well with the suggestion that ideology tends to appear in a poor light simply because Marx is almost exclusively concerned with ideological beliefs which he rejects. Some extra light is shed on the particular case by the later return to the theme of the 'great revolution of society brought about by competition'.[7] On this occasion Marx draws attention to the way it 'destroyed for the proletarians all naturally derived and traditional relations, e.g., family and political relations, together with their entire ideological super-structure'. It is hard to detect a hint here that there is something necessarily amiss with the ideological super-structure of the proletarians. Indeed, in view of Marx's respect for it and for natural and traditional relations generally, the critical drift might well be supposed to be the other way. At any rate one must surely be the slave of a theory to insist on reading a sense of cognitive stigma into references such as these.

There are others in *The German Ideology* which might be regarded as more promising. Thus, one hears a good deal on such topics as 'ideological deception', 'ideological dis-tortion', and 'the illusions of the ideologists'.[8] It was suggested above that the frequency of such references may be explained by the particular circumstances of the work. It should now be added that so far from lending support to the epistemological thesis, it constitutes rather a problem for it to solve. For if it is correct, the references turn out to have a pleonastic character, and on a scale that would be quite uncharacteristic in Marx. It might perhaps be said that they are saved from complete redundancy through a concern, on the occasions of their use, to contrast ideological and non-ideological kinds of error. But the suggestion does not fit the particular cases very well, and relies on a distinction which has little resonance in Marx's work in general. It seems more reasonable to suppose that these cases rely for their point rather on the contrast with the many 'neutral' references to ideological matters; to, for instance, ideolog-ical 'theories', 'postulates' and 'methods' and to 'the thoughts and ideas of the ideologists'.[9] Marx can make use of this contrast precisely because he does not conceive of ideology as necessarily connected with cognitive defect. Thus, the very frequency of the references to ideological error suggests that it cannot be a conceptual truth about ideology that it is erroneous.

The focus of the discussion may now be narrowed still further. So far it has served to suggest that the great bulk of the evidence in *The German Ideology* is readily compatible with, or lends active support to, our thesis. It should be noted, however, that exponents of the epistemological doctrine seldom trouble to range over the work as a whole, or even substantial portions of it, in their search for support. All too often they rest content with a single passage which is taken as decisively settling the issue by itself. Of course, too much account need not be taken of isolated quotations which are in opposition to the main body of evidence. Nevertheless, the passage in question has traditionally been accorded a great deal of significance. It does not seem adequately dealt with by the arguments advanced so far, and might well be regarded as constituting a genuine *prima facie* difficulty for our thesis. At any rate it constitutes the last serious obstacle in the way of assimilating the work as a whole and as such deserves consideration in some detail. The passage is the well-known one containing the metaphor of the *camera obscura*.

It may help in getting our initial bearings to quote from the standard translation we have been using up to now:

> Men are the producers of their conceptions, ideas, etc.—real, active men, as they are conditioned by a definite development of their productive forces and of the intercourse corresponding to these, up to its furthest forms. Consciousness can never be anything else than conscious existence, and the existence of men is their actual life-process. If in all ideology men and their circumstances appear upside-down as in a *camera obscura*, this phenomenon arises just as much from their historical life-process as the inversion of objects on the retina does from their physical life-process.
>
> In direct contrast to German philosophy which descends from heaven to earth, here we ascend from earth to heaven.[10]

This is, it should be said, one of the passages in Marx most often treated as a source of 'isolated aphorisms'. In the light of our earlier warnings, it is important not to be satisfied with such a treatment, but to insist on seeing it in the context of the work as a whole. The main features of the context have already been sketched. The work is primarily a critique of 'German criticism' which has 'right up to its latest efforts, never quitted the realm of philosophy', and specifically that of the Hegelian philosophy.[11] Marx's overriding concern, as was remarked earlier, is with the persistence of the idealist ontology, the primacy in the world accorded to concepts. In developing the case he provides, as is conventionally said, the first major exposition of the materialist world-outlook. The main theme of the exposition, recurring again and again with variations of detail, is the idea most aphoristically expressed in the saying 'Life is not determined by consciousness, but consciousness by life.' This formulation occurs just after the passage we are concerned with, but the theme itself is already dominant there and is overtly present in the earlier part which provides the immediate background to the *camera obscura* reference. As questions of translation will, of necessity, be of some significance in the discussion, it may be well to cite the sentence in which the reference appears in its original form. It runs as follows:

> Wenn in der ganzen Ideologie die Menschen und ihre Verhältnisse wie in einer Camera obscura auf den Kopf gestellt erscheinen, so geht dies Phänomen ebensosehr aus ihrem historischen Lebens-prozess hervor, wie die Umdrehung der Gegenstände auf der Netzhaut aus ihrem unmittelbar physischen.[12]

A crucial point to attend to here is the rendering of the phrase '*in der ganzen Ideologie*' as 'in all ideology'.[13] The use in the original of the definite article with an adjective might rather be taken to suggest that it is some particular ideology that is in question. Hence, it might be thought more natural to translate it as, simply, 'in the whole ideology'. If this version were adopted the only possible referent would be the 'German' or 'Hegelian' ideology. Such a reading fits perfectly with the chief preoccupation of the work as a whole, and, more significantly, is supported by features of the immediate context. In particular, one should note the use of the phrase 'upside-down' (*auf den Kopf gestellt*). This is not to be taken as a vague, umbrella expression for things going awry or being misconceived in a general sort of way. The image of things upside-down, placed on their heads, is a favourite recourse with Marx when he wishes specifically to characterize his relationship with Hegelianism. It crops up in this connection in *The Holy Family* and, perhaps the best-known instance, in an 'Afterword' to *Capital*, as well as elsewhere in *The German Ideology*.[14] It is significant that these usages may in their turn be regarded as deliberate echoes of phrases from Hegel's own writings; most obviously, from the 'Preface' to the *Phenomenology*.[15] We are dealing with a device which Marx found congenial in a certain context to denote a determinate kind of mis-conception, and this fact in itself tells against the assumption that its use here is part of a general characterization of ideology. It is intended rather to point to the central Hegelian doctrine that is under attack in *The German Ideology*, the reversal of the true order of priority of consciousness and material reality. The sentence that immediately follows shows that the descent from heaven to earth in German philosophy is right at the forefront of Marx's attention at this stage, and so bears out the contextual appropriateness of our reading. The point he wishes to make might now be paraphrased as follows:

> If in the German ideology as a whole the primacy of material life over consciousness is reversed, still this phenomenon itself arises from the real conditions of historical existence and is susceptible to a materialist explanation.

This interpretation accords well with the idea that the main theoretical achievement of the work is its explanation of materialism. Read in such a way it is obvious that the *camera obscura* passage presents no difficulty whatever for our thesis.

It is, however, not easy to feel satisfied that matters may simply be left like this. For one thing our discussion has the effect of placing other features of the familiar translation in a new light. Thus, it might be thought slightly surprising that Marx should have felt the need at this stage to present his view of the upside-down character of the German ideology in the shape of a hypothesis. In this connection it may be well to bear in mind that the rendering of *'wenn'* as 'if', while no doubt legitimate, is not actually obligatory here. Indeed, it may be preferable to recognize its role as concessionary rather than suppositional in character, with something of the force of 'given that . . . '. In following up this suggestion the sentence may be recast in the following sort of way:

> The phenomenon that in the whole ideology men and their circumstances appear upside-down as in a *camera obscura* arises just as much from their historical life-process as the inversion of objects on the retina does from their physical life-process.

This reading has the merit of testifying in the clearest way to the conclusion that Marx's prime concern is to bring the insights of materialism to bear on a specific ideological phenomenon of the time. But, as we have seen, the same general point can be made through the use of the hypothetical form, and in truth nothing of consequence for our argument hinges on whether that form is retained. Much more important are some misgivings that may remain concerning the contextual appropriateness of the phrase 'in the whole ideology', regardless of how the surrounding sentence is structured. For it may be thought not to fit as smoothly as one could wish with what immediately precedes it in the passage. It is true that the theme being pursued there, the relationship of existence and consciousness, is fully in keeping with our reading in a general way. Nevertheless, the phrase may still be experienced as signalling a switch to a new level of particularity with an abruptness that gives one something of a jolt. In itself this consideration is by no means decisive. Smoothness of texture is not a notable feature of Marx's work. Sudden transitions do occur in it, as, indeed, they do in writers whose manner is less energetic and abrasive. Moreover, the text we have of *The German Ideology* is particularly illustrative of the tendency. The point involved is, nevertheless, serious enough to encourage one to look for a reading that will remove any sense of unease while continuing to do justice to the original impression of a certain degree of specificity of reference. A natural suggestion is that one might be able to interpret the focus of concern not as one particular ideology but as any individual ideology as such. It should be possible to achieve this while remaining sensitive to the linguistic pressures of the text. Some such formula as 'in the whole body (or "the totality") of an ideology' seems to be indicated. For convenience in using it one has to return to the hypothetical structure of the standard translation. The consequent of the statement remains as before, but its purpose now is to guarantee the possibility of a materialist explanation not just where the entire German ideology gets things upside-down, but in the case of any ideology that fully shares the German upside-downness. This represents a more substantial claim and one that is, perhaps, more appropriate to the stage reached in the discussion. Hence, it may well constitute a better reading, one that more adequately captures the shade of meaning that Marx had in mind. But, of course, it offers as little encouragement as do our previous suggestions to any tendency to view ideology, as such, as a cognitively-deficient category.

So far the discussion has served to suggest that in this case the standard translation should be treated with caution. It does not attempt a literal rendering, but embodies an element of interpretation in a stronger sense that one has to accept as normal or inevitable. The element stands in need of justification which could only be supplied by drawing on some larger assumptions about the nature of Marx's concern with the ideological. This is the point to be emphasized for purposes of the present discussion. The translation may be said to presuppose the epistemological thesis, but it does not provide any independent support for it. As the thesis can rely on no such support from elsewhere in Marx, the flimsiness of its foundations now stands clearly revealed. It would, however, be misleading to leave the impression that issues of translation are crucial at this stage of our argument: it is, fortunately, not dependent on any scholarly claims, however modest, in the way that would suggest. The standard translation is indeed tendentious and makes it difficult to see what is at issue but, given an adequate discussion, no dire consequences need follow on its acceptance. That is to say, even if it is allowed that the referent is ideology as such, 'all ideology', and if, as a corollary, the statement is explicitly cast in the hypothetical mode, our view of the general point of the passage will not need to be significantly revised. To bring this out, one may adopt the procedure most favoured by supporters of the epistemological doctrine, and concentrate attention on the antecedent clause by itself: 'in all ideology men and their circumstances appear upside-down as in a *camera obscura*'.[16] This has now to be considered as a theoretical statement about the nature of ideology. On general grounds it might be thought unlikely that Marx would wish to be committed to an image with so much specificity as the emblem of the ideological realm. Such misgivings are greatly reinforced if one bears in mind what was said above about the particular associations the image has in his work. There is no good reason to saddle him with the view that all ideology has inevitably a Hegelian-idealist character. In a previous chapter it was argued that this attribution fails to take account of important areas of his practice and would considerably reduce the value of the concept for theoretical inquiry.[17] It may be added that supporters of the epistemological doctrine do not usually seem to want to tie their interpretation down in any such manner: the usual aim is to let ideology denote not a particular style of error but a mode of cognition that is defective in some more pervasive way. At any rate the point is that the claim represented by the antecedent as stated above would quite certainly have been regarded by Marx as false: it is not his view that ideology necessarily partakes of the Hegelian reversal of existence and consciousness. If one recalls the hypothetical character of the statement as a whole, it now has to be recognized that what one is dealing with is an unfulfilled or contrary-to-fact conditional, a conterfactual in the current jargon. This is a standard and obvious device for illustrating the explanatory force of a scientific hypothesis by showing how it would apply in circumstances that have not in fact been realized. What Marx may be presumed to have had in mind on this interpretation could be brought out in the following sort of way: 'Even if, as is not the case, all ideology had an idealist character, still that fact too could be explained on the materialist hypothesis.' The point would be that even idealism has a material base: the seemingly frictionless descent from heaven is in reality a laborious product of earth. Once again the explanatory thrust of the statement, such as it is, is seen to be directed towards Marx's materialism rather than his conception of ideology. It is perhaps ironic that the standard translation, by forcing the conterfactual interpretation on us, should bring this out even more decisively than do the alternatives suggested above. But whichever reading one cares to adopt, it is clear that the threat to our thesis from the *camera obscura* passage has vanished. By displaying its true significance in the argument we have removed any temptation to suppose that a definition of ideology is being canvassed there. In particular, it is not the case that it attempts to establish any theoretical connection with error or illusion. This apparently awkward case now slips with ease into the perspective on the work that was suggested earlier, and with it the last obstacle in the text has disappeared. Marx's aim in *The German Ideology* is to unmask some powerful tendencies in the ideological world of the time. The frequency with which their defects are pointed out should not, however, be allowed to invade one's sense of what is essential to his conception of ideology. What that is lies beneath the surface here as elsewhere, and when it is recovered turns out to be in no way unique. So far as the treatment of ideology is concerned, the text does not constitute an anomaly of any kind in the pattern of the life-work as a whole.

A question that now presses even more strongly than before is why it is that the nature of the pattern has been so widely misconceived. In particular, one must ask how to account for the prevalence of the assumption that for Marx ideology has a distinctive epistemological status. Any serious attempt to do so will have to respect the scale of the phenomenon by working on a variety of levels. It is clear, however, that at some point reference has to be made to the role of Engels in mediating the original body of thought. It is true that on the whole his dealings with the ideological fit readily within the thesis of this essay. For one thing, that thesis has been developed, at least in part, on the basis of works of which he was co-author with Marx. While there can be little doubt as to whose is the dominant intellectual influence, there is no reason to suppose that either felt any discomfort with the views they express.[18] Moreover, the writings of Engels after Marx's death contain many striking formulations of the authentic doctrine. Thus, for instance, in the 'Preface' of 1885 to the third German edition of *The Eighteenth Brumaire* he refers to Marx's discovery of 'the great law of motion of history, the law according to which all historical struggles, whether they proceed in the political, religious, philosophical or some other ideological domain, are in fact only the more or less clear expression of struggles of social classes'.[19] The ideological domains constitute, it appears, a medium for the expression of class struggles. This, of course, takes one to the heart of the Marxist conception, and Engels may be seen as providing here a more explicit version of the formula of the 1859 'Preface', incorporating the same suggestion of indifference to the cognitive status of the warring ideas. Elsewhere, when he puts the notion of ideology to concrete use in historical analysis, it is the role of ideas in serving class interests that holds the centre of the stage. The discussion of the ideological significance of religion in *Ludwig Feuerbach* (1888) may serve as an illustration:

> The Middle Ages had attached to theology all the other forms of ideology—philosophy, politics, jurisprudence—and made them subdivisions of theology. It thereby constrained every social and political movement to take on a theological form. The sentiments of the masses were fed with religion to the exclusion of all else; it was therefore necessary to put forward their own interests in a religious guise in order to produce an impetuous movement.[20]

Engels goes on to remark how, at a later stage:

> . . . the Calvinist Reformation . . . provided the ideological costume for the second act of the bourgeois revolution, which was taking place in England. Here Calvinism justified itself as the true religious disguise of the interests of the bourgeoisie of that time. . . .[21]

Later still, when 'Christianity entered into its final stage', it became 'incapable for the future of serving any progressive class as the ideological garb of its aspirations'. Instead, it 'became more and more the exclusive possession of the ruling classes and these apply it as a mere means of government, to keep the lower classes within bounds'.[22] It is clear that this entire discussion is directly founded on the premise of the classical Marxist conception of ideology. Its ruling assumption is that the serving of class interests is the *raison d'être* of the ideological realm and that recognition of this fact is constitutive of the standpoint of ideological analysis.

It would be possible at this point to go through the rest of the work produced for publication by Engels in order to show in detail the congruence between his treatment of the ideological and that of Marx. In doing so one might, of course, have to recognize some differences of emphasis. It might have to be said, for instance, that the settling of accounts in *The German Ideology* proved less conclusive in Engels's case. At any rate, his ideological concerns continued to revolve to a significantly greater extent around the German idealist philosophy. To put the point at its strongest, this body of work may be said to have gone on providing for him the paradigms of bourgeois ideology while Marx, as we have noted, was to shift his main attention elsewhere. Thus, in *Anti-Dühring* the 'old favourite ideological method' is still 'the *a priori* method' which 'consists in ascertaining the properties of an object, by logical deduction from the concept of the object, instead of from the object itself '.[23] This enduring concern with the shortcomings of idealism may reflect a taste for metaphysics not sustained by Marx. On the other hand it may be that the impression of a contrast simply results from the division of intellectual labour that grew up between them in later years.[24] It is natural enough that this particular case should reveal the influence of old habits of thought, since the analysis of *The German Ideology* applies in all essentials to Dühring also:

> Herr Dühring dare not designate thought as being human, and so he has to sever it from the only real foundation on which we find it, namely, man and nature; and with that he tumbles hopelessly into an ideology which reveals him as the epigone of the 'epigone' Hegel.[25]

Whatever the explanation, it seems clear that this ideology continued to function in a more central role for Engels than for Marx. But the difference is one that affects primarily the choice of subjects for analysis, and there would seem to be no good grounds for allotting it any larger theoretical significance. Even if this were accepted, however, and the programme of piecemeal scrutiny of everything Engels wrote for publication were successfully carried out, it must be admitted that our problem would not then disappear. For the discussion so far has failed to touch the core of it. This is best captured in a formula that is perhaps the most familiar expression of the epistemological thesis; ideology is or involves, it is said, a 'false consciousness'. Such a view is attributed over and over again by commentators to Engels, and to Marx also, often without any attempt to supply argument or evidence.[26] The slogan may therefore serve to crystallize the residual difficulties that the thesis presents, and these can only be disposed of if it is tackled directly.

The crucial point to note is the slightness of its textual base. The phrase 'false consciousness' does not occur in Marx, and the only significant support for its use in the slogan consists in some comments made in a letter, written ten years after his death, from Engels to Franz Mehring:

> Ideology is a process accomplished by the so-called thinker consciously, it is true, but with a false consciousness. The real motive forces impelling him remain unknown to him; otherwise it simply would not be an ideological process. Hence he imagines false or seeming motive forces.[27]

It is hard to see how this can be taken at anything like face value. Ideology for Marx, and for Engels elsewhere, is an objective social phenomenon grounded in and guaranteed by the existence of classes. Its secret is not to be found in the blindness of individuals to the 'motive forces' of their thinking. Where such a suggestion naturally leads is towards the elaboration of theories of ideology along psycho-analytical or existentialist lines. Within the classical Marxist framework ideology cannot be identified with any kind of self-deception, rationalization or bad faith, and is not to be removed by therapy directed at such conditions. It might be tempting to try to stay within that framework by, as it were, de-psychologizing what Engels says while preserving something of the original idea. It then becomes a conception not of ignorance of 'motive forces' but of failure to grasp the theoretical presuppositions of one's thinking. The suggestion made by Althusser that ideology is marked by unconsciousness of its problematic may perhaps be viewed as a development along those lines, and no doubt it owes something to the influence of the Mehring letter.[28] It is, however, as we have seen, open to serious objection; in particular of failing to accommodate the practico-social aspect of ideology. It is not pursued with any enthusiasm by Althusser himself, and generally the line of thought involved has found little favour among commentators inside or outside Marxism. Far more common has been the tendency simply to ignore the specific suggestion of lack of insight into the basis of thought. The phrase 'false consciousness' has instead been lifted completely out of its original context and used as a general synonym for error or deception. It has thus passed into intellectual currency without any regard for the particular shade of meaning that Engels wished to attach to it. Such a development cannot, of course, claim even so much of the authority of his name as would otherwise attach to the contents of the Mehring letter. That is to say, it has no roots at all in the writings of the founders of Marxism. If this generalized notion of 'false consciousness' is combined with the wish to accommodate the social dimension of ideology, one may be led still further from any position held by Engels. The combination has all too often come about within the ambit of the kind of empiricism discussed in the previous chapter. Hence, it finds expression in the form of writing certain requirements about the social distribution of the defective forms of consciousness into the concept of ideology. By this route one arrives at the kind of definition conventionally associated with Marx and Marxism in textbooks and works of reference: 'a false consciousness of social and economic realities, a collective illusion shared by the members of a given social class and in history distinctively associated with that class'.[29] The whole thrust of our argument has been to show that this account is fundamentally mistaken. There is a sad irony in the fact that it should be necessary to link the reputation and influence of Engels, however indirectly and adventitiously, with such a travesty. To do them justice it may be best to focus on the significance of his career as a whole, and treat the remarks on 'false consciousness' as an aberration, an instance of that curious uncertainty of touch he could sometimes display, even on matters supposedly central to doctrines held jointly with Marx. It is all the more easy to take such a view if one bears in mind the distinction he himself drew between the standards appropriate to published work and to private correspondence. Some six months after the Mehring letter he was to advise another correspondent: 'Please do not weigh each word in the above too scrupulously, but keep the general connection in mind; I regret that I have not the time to word what I am writing to you exactly as I should be obliged to do for publication ...'.[30] This suggests very well the kind of perspective in which that letter should be viewed. In doing so, it helps to bring out how slight was the impulse originally given to the hare of 'false consciousness' which has been running so vigorously ever since. It must also reinforce the determination not to allow a large part of the significance of a person's life and work to be destroyed by a phrase.

When the fog of the epistemological doctrine has lifted, a number of issues can be seen to fall into their proper place. Prominent among them is that of 'the end of ideology'. The discussion has already noted Althusser's rejection of the 'utopian idea' of a world from which ideology has disappeared and his denial that historical materialism can conceive of even a communist society in those terms.[31] It should now be clear in what way this view is mistaken. For not merely is historical materialism able to conceive of such a situation, but its feasibility is an integral part of the doctrine of the founders. The real world of ideology is class society and class conflict, and it disappears from the historical stage with the close of the epoch which is characterized by those conditions. But since it is not to be identified with any particular level of cognitive achievement, this disappearance has in itself no epistemological significance. The image of the end of ideology is that of the situation in which the primary social conflict has been resolved and in which, as a result, the intellectual medium of its existence has lost its function. This is not an extra, utopian element tacked onto the idea of the communist society: it is part of the specification of that society. A Marxist may entertain a rational hope that the end of ideology will be accompanied by the dissemination of higher forms of consciousness than obtain in class society. The historical preconditions of the two are, after all, to a large extent identical. Thus, for instance, a rich source of pollution is removed with the loss of the ability of the old ruling class to hire its prizefighters. The hope may be reinforced by drawing on other resources in Marx's thought, on such themes as the end of alienation and of the fetishism of commodities, the conquest of the realm of freedom or the reversal of the previous order of consciousness and social existence. What Marx and Engels dismiss as 'utopian' are attempts to work out the implications of these themes for the future society in any detail. Their own suggestions as to the nature of the consciousness that will characterize it are of the vaguest and most tentative kind. Nothing in what they say, however, gives any grounds for supposing that in it individuals will enjoy a complete transparency of their relationships, or that their lives will be wholly free of the effects of ignorance, irrationality or narrowness of sympathies. There is no reason to doubt that they will go on being deceivers and self-deceivers, victims of anxiety, guilt, despair and the other dark forces that constitute the interest of 'the human condition' for some observers. All one can say is that whatever forms of illusion flourish in the communist society they will not be ideological; that is, they will not serve the needs of structural contradictions in the social formation. To say this is to point to one of the preconditions of a truly human society, one that does not, by its nature, systematically obstruct the attempts of the mass of its members to cope with the burdens of being human. It is not a vision of 'men like gods' from whom these burdens have been lifted. It may be that Althusser's stance derives from a commendable anxiety to protect Marxism from the suspicion of falling into a shallow rationalism on this issue. But if so it shows the error of his controlling assumptions. When the epistemological connection is given up, it becomes clear that 'the end of ideology' involves no such risk.

There is an aspect of those assumptions that should be particularly noted here. One reason for Althusser's insistence that human beings must live in ideology is that for him the only conceivable alternative is that they should live in science. Hence, a significant feature of his stance is the way it illustrates the pernicious consequences of the ideology-science dichotomy. This too may now be laid finally to rest.

The recognition that ideology is not, while science inescapably is, a category of epistemological import is the first step to understanding here. It enables one to see why the question, 'what is the nature of the distinction between science and ideology?' generates no fruitful lines of inquiry in Marxist theory. The reason is that the concepts involved are of different logical types and the attempt to treat them as though they might form the basis of a taxonomy is a symptom of confusion. It may be helpful at this point to focus on a concrete case. On Marx's view of the matter, one seems obliged to recognize that Ricardo's work somehow partakes of the status both of ideology and of science. Yet it should not be assumed on that account that together they must constitute a grid to be laid down on it, so that the one could be seen to begin where the other leaves off. This would be to misconceive the way the categories have application. Its ideological character belongs to the system as a whole, pervading its entire structure. This is so in virtue of the fact that, as Marx never tires of remarking, it is wholly conceived from the vantage point of capitalist production, which is assumed to be the natural, eternally valid, human mode. It could only vulgarize his notion of ideology to attempt to operate with it inside the system, as a way of identifying the less reputable elements. For that, one simply needs a conception of degrees of scientific merit and, perhaps, a distinction between science and non-science or pseudo-science. An attempt to impose a science-ideology dichotomy here would suggest a failure to make adequate discriminations among the forms of social consciousness as he depicts them.

It was earlier suggested that the theme of ideology should be separated from that of class consciousness. Both have now to be distinguished from the question of what is involved in understanding society, from the idea of a social science. Marx offers no ready-made, theoretically adequate account of this theme either. From the scattered references to it, one may assume that such a science must have a dialectical character, and would generally involve the penetration of appearances to the reality beneath. The results of such a process of dialectical penetration will, no doubt, be of ideological significance in class society and questions of great interest arise in that connection. They cannot begin to be answered, however, without a sense of the basic conceptual configurations. The minimum requirement is to recognise the radical heterogeneity of the concepts of ideology, class consciousness and social science, and to give up hope of mapping their interrelations neatly on a single plane. But this, of course, is not the end of the matter. Having insisted on the need to make distinctions, we shall at a later stage have to face the task of reconstituting the unity of Marx's thought by showing something of the complex pattern in which it holds their elements together.

For the present we may continue to reap the more immediate benefits of giving up the polar opposition of science and ideology. Most obviously perhaps, it puts us in a position to return and deal with the question of the ideological significance of the natural sciences. The assumption that in the very act of posing it one must be raising doubts about cognitive status is a serious hindrance to inquiry. Yet the issues involved here are of great importance, and were seen as such by the founders of the classical Marxist tradition of ideology. Thus, a persistent concern in *History and Class Consciousness* is the complicated symbiosis in bourgeois thought between conceptions of nature and of society, Lukács sees that 'there is something highly problematic in the fact that capitalist society is predisposed to harmonize with scientific method'.[32] The first step in solving the problem is to grasp that 'nature is a societal category'.[33] Hence it is that under capitalism the 'natural laws' of society 'have the task of subordinating the categories of nature to the process of socialisation'.[34] Tönnies is quoted to illustrate one aspect of the situation that results:

> . . . scientific concepts . . . behave within science like commodities in society. They gather together within the system like commodities on the market.[35]

The other aspect of this relationship appears when one considers how the theoretical understanding of society is, in its turn, pervaded by the modes of thought of natural science. Lukács insists that 'Every such "atomic" theory of society only represents the ideological reflection of the purely bourgeois point of view'.[36] Thus, bourgeois thought is characterized by the belief that the real motor forces of history 'belong, as it were, to nature and that in them and in their causal interactions it is possible to discern the "eternal" laws of nature'.[37] The implications for ideological analysis are spelled out in the discussion of Engels's proof that force (law and the state) 'was originally grounded in an economic social function'. This, Lukács comments:

> . . . must be interpreted to mean—in strict accordance with the theories of Marx and Engels—that in consequence of this connection a corresponding ideological picture is found projected into the thoughts and feelings of men who are drawn into the ambit of authority. That is to say, the organs of authority harmonize to such an extent with the (economic) laws governing men's lives, or seem so overwhelmingly superior that men experience them as natural forces, as the necessary environment for their existence. As

a result they submit to them *freely*. (Which is not to say that they *approve* of them.)[38]

The general conclusion to be drawn here is that, on Lukács's view, the main axis of bourgeois thought is the conception of a unified science of nature and society. The ideological function of this conception is to confirm the tendency to experience the institutions of bourgeois society as forces of nature, to confer on them the ontological solidity of the forms of the physical universe itself. The process at work is essentially the same as that encountered in the discussion of the Australian aborigines, the conceptual underpinning of social arrangements through the projection of their image onto the universe at large. Hence, it is the second, 'syntactic' model of ideology that is the appropriate instrument for explicating it. The search for ideologically significant evaluations among the propositions and theories of natural science is, in any case, likely to be of marginal interest, and runs the risk of trivializing the issues at stake. It is hardly surprising that of the major figures of classical Marxism it should be Lukács who provides the most direct help in doing them justice. On his own account, he had originally been drawn to Marx 'the sociologist' under the influence of Weber,[39] and clearly the methodological lesson of *The Protestant Ethic* has been thoroughly assimilated by him:

> . . . it is no accident that it was the revolutionary religiosity of the sects that supplied the ideology for capitalism in its purest forms (in England and America). For the union of an inwardness, purified to the point of total abstraction and stripped of all traces of flesh and blood, with a transcendental philosophy of history does indeed correspond to the basic ideological structure of capitalism.[40]

It is precisely our contention that where the ideological significance of natural science is concerned it is primarily with correspondences between structures that one has to deal. The language used by Lukács of 'harmonizing', 'reflecting' and 'projecting corresponding ideological pictures' is perfectly adapted to exploring such a theme. His own exploration displays a sharp awareness that among the pictures which bourgeois society projects into the thoughts and feelings of men, its picture of the natural world has a distinctive place. For it is uniquely suited to holding them captive through the effect of inexorable repetition. Its scope and authority ensure for it a special role in reassuring the bourgeois that the world is his world and in encouraging others to feel at home in it too, or at least to experience their alienation as a kind of deviance.

It was suggested earlier that the ideological relevance of natural science was not lost on the founders of the Marxist tradition. This is perhaps best evidenced by the way in which the need to come to terms with it supplies so much of the pressure behind the debate over the dialectics of nature. In *History and Class Consciousness* the dialectical categories are interpreted in a way that makes it impossible to see how they could apply outside human society. This consequence is frankly acknowledged by Lukács,[41] and, indeed, he gives the impression of wholly conceding the validity of the non-dialectical mode of inquiry in its own sphere:

> When the ideal of scientific knowledge is applied to nature it simply furthers the progress of science. But when it is applied to society it turns out to be an ideological weapon of the bourgeoisie.[42]

His response to the situation is to give up the idea of a unified science. This is, in effect, to admit the affinity between natural science and bourgeois society, and then concentrate on drawing its ideological sting. By marking society sharply off from nature he seeks, as it were, to put the world-view of natural science in quarantine. This approach is consciously opposed to that adopted in Engels's treatment of the subject. There the strategy is rather to restore the idea of a unified science from a different viewpoint, to obliterate the connection between natural science and capitalism by reclaiming the study of nature for the materialist dialectic. The two positions are the main poles of reference in a debate

that has continued ever since within Marxism. To understand it, one has to see that the issues at stake are not just of
theoretical interest, but have, and were experienced by the
participants as having, the largest ideological significance.
Viewed in that perspective, the driving force of the debate is
the wish to deprive bourgeois society of the intellectual
authority of science. The need arises from the fact that
capitalism and modern science have grown up together in the
same environment and share its structural imprint. It is all
the more pressing in that in this environment the systematic
study of nature had come to be thought of as supplying the
paradigms of human knowledge and rationality in general.
But of course, as the Australian case reminds one, images of
the non-human world are likely to have a fundamental
significance for the process of legitimation in any society.

It is through the 'syntactic' model that their significance
has to be made manifest. The value of the model is, however,
by no means confined to this range of cases. There is not
space here to develop the possibilities in detail, but
something may be said to illustrate them. It will be
convenient to stay with the intellectual projections of
bourgeois society, where Lukács may once again serve as a
guide. The 'atomisation of society', he remarks, must 'have a
profound influence on the thought, the science and the
philosophy of capitalism'.[43] In *History and Class Consciousness* this influence is most fully explored in connection with the tradition of classical German philosophy.
The treatment of it as the 'complete intellectual copy' of
bourgeois society demonstrates very well the possibilities
we have in mind.[44] The theme may be expanded a little by
considering a philosopher whose career offers a remarkable
postscript to Lukács's account. Wittgenstein is conventionally enough regarded as the heir of Kant and
Schopenhauer who takes the natural logic of their position to
its furthest limit. In this achievement, one may say, lies the
source of his exemplary significance for the ideological
analysis of bourgeois society. His work deserves, of course,

to be viewed as more than just a case study in such an analysis. As one might expect of a thinker obsessed throughout his life with the 'pictoriality of thought',[45] it is also a rich source of methodological insight so far as the second model of ideology is concerned. Some echoes from it have, almost inevitably, already crept into the discussion here. In the *Tractatus* the treatment of the central issue of the relationship between language and the world rests on the most uncompromising assertion of structural identity that could be imagined. It is tempting to propose a measure of analogy between the operation of the elementary propositions as pictures which share the logical form of their subjects and that of the ideological complexes with their homology of structures. To do so should enable one to benefit from Wittgenstein's treatment of the pictorial relationship, at least as a classic statement of one way of conceiving it. In the present discussion, however, we must be content with applying what methodological insights we have to the substantive thesis of the work. Its ontology, the view of the world as the totality of atomic facts which are themselves configurations of simple objects, is surely to be seen as the most refined theoretical expression of the atomizing tendencies of bourgeois society, its complete intellectual copy in the realm of metaphysics. The interest of the theory for ideological inquiry is not in any way diminished by the innocence of its author's intentions, nor by the level of abstraction which rules out any suggestion of a practico-social role. It is these very features which constitute it as so pure an illustration of the basic ideological process of the reproduction of the structures of a society in thought. Such a case brings home all the more vividly the fact that the patterns in terms of which the society is conceived will be found congenial and authoritative over a wide field of intellectual life. Thus, it helps one to see how the ideology that is the medium for the images of bourgeois society may come to permeate the consciousness of an epoch.

So far the discussion has dealt in connections which, though important, are fairly bald and schematic. More satisfying are the possibilities of linking Wittgenstein to the ideological analysis of classical bourgeois philosophy at lower levels of detail. They arise, for instance, in regard to that question of 'the irrational', which is, for Lukács, the crux and solvent of the whole tradition.[46] The *Tractatus* exemplifies very clearly one kind of response to it with which he has made us familiar, the combination of the most complete refinement of rational technique in matters of detail with a blank irrationality as regards the whole.[47] This is, on Lukács's account, an inescapable feature of bourgeois thought, imposed by the objective limits and internal contradictions of bourgeois society. What is remarkable in Wittgenstein is the frankness with which a virtue is made of necessity. The acceptance of the unintelligibility of the whole, the loss of intellectual control at this point, is celebrated as the most profound wisdom. The feeling for the world as a whole is explicitly identified with 'the mystical', and the sense of this world is located outside it in the region which one cannot speak of but must consign to silence.[48] The stoically tragic attitude in the face of the unknowable that Lukács admired in Kant has now degenerated into an enervate mysticism. To say this is not to compare the merits of individual thinkers as such, but rather to register the decline of a tradition of thought and, behind that, the changing fortunes of a class and of the society it dominated.

The working out of the process may be pursued in the later Wittgenstein. At one point, in discussing the treatment by some bourgeois thinkers of 'the unsolved problem of the irrational' and the way it 'reappears in the problem of totality', Lukács comments:

> The horizon that delimits the totality that has been and can be created here is, at best, culture (i.e. the culture of bourgeois society). This culture cannot be derived from anything else and has simply to be accepted on its own terms as 'facticity' in the sense given to it by the classical philosophers.[49]

It is surely difficult, coming on this in the present context, not to hear some further echoes: 'What has to be accepted, the given, is—so one could say—*forms of life*.'[50] The value of Lukács's comment is that it enforces a recognition of some simple truths. The forms that have to be accepted must, in practice, turn out to be the forms of bourgeois society. Hence, by investing them with authority Wittgenstein's dictum involves a politically significant kind of conservatism. The history of the reception of the later work, in particular the use made of it in social theory by the 'Wittgensteinians', fits well with this conclusion. The main point to note, however, is that the movement traced here between the sense of cosmic ineffability and the determination to cling to the immediacy of the socially given is characteristic of a tendency which goes deep in bourgeois thought and has considerable ideological significance. To note it is to be reminded both of the exemplary value of Wittgenstein's career and of the acuteness of Lukács's perception of the intellectual needs and resources of bourgeois society.[51]

It is not possible in this essay to deal with all the varieties of confusion that flow from the epistemological doctrine. There is, however, one other line of development which deserves attention in order to clarify some aspects of our own position. It may be introduced by referring again to the misreading of *The German Ideology* which sees the links between ideology and cognitive defect as peculiarly tight there, and claims a contrast in this respect with the later work. Althusser again provides a convenient illustration. In *The German Ideology*, he remarks, 'Ideology is conceived as a pure illusion, a pure dream, i.e. as nothingness.'[52] Such a conception is, of course, impossible to reconcile with his sense of its massive and inescapable presence in social formations. Indeed, it is hard to see how it could permit any serious attempt to do justice to the practico-social dimension. On the other hand, there are, as we have seen, no good grounds for attributing it to Marx at any stage of his career.

If, however, *The German Ideology* is read and rejected in this way, one may easily be led, under the auspices of the epistemological doctrine, to try to define a more satisfactory cognitive status for ideology. This may be seen as an attempt to uncover the mature view of Marx. It will have to operate with a rather more complicated scheme than that represented by the ideology-science dichotomy. Its poles of reference will be constituted by science at one extreme and 'pure illusion' at the other, and the object will be to mark out a location for ideology somewhere in between. A good deal of recent discussion under Althusserian influence has been based on this problematic.[53] It is difficult, however, to see how anything worthwhile can come of it. The programme is vitiated by its combination of the epistemological thesis with essentialist assumptions about meaning. Ideology, it is supposed, must be assigned as a unified whole to a particular place in the epistemological spectrum. Its essence lies in the occupation of that place, in that specific kind of cognitive relation to reality that is the ideological relation. But even if the technical difficulties involved in staking out a plausible intermediate site were overcome, the identification of it with ideology would be merely gratuitous. At least it derives no warrant from the classical Marxist tradition, and could only be a source of tension in the work of anyone who wished to retain some organic link with it. In that tradition ideology figures as the intellectual powerhouse of the class struggle. To carry out this function it must involve or make possible for subscribers some more or less reliable orientation towards reality. Its success in its social role is indeed inexplicable if it is thought of as pure illusion. But recognition of this can be accommodated without introducing any new varieties into the overgrown garden of epistemology. It is not necessary that ideology as such should represent a distinctive cognitive achievement falling somewhere between knowledge in the full sense and mere fantasy, that there should be a particular kind of cognitive relation to the world that is the ideological relation. What is needed, one might say, is to take one's terms distributively and not collectively in this case. It is necessary that some proportion, and how high cannot be specified in advance, of ideological forms should be veridical in their particular social context. Powerful and long-established ideologies, such as that of the bourgeoisie in contemporary capitalism, are bound to have substantial cognitive merits. These are facts which the classical Marxist conception of ideology as thought which serves class interests is well able to accommodate. It supplies the principle of unity which binds together the immensely varied forms of bourgeois ideology in their extraordinary mixture of truth and error, transparence and opacity, insight and illusion. The assumption that ideology must itself be seen as a distinctive epistemological category is a strategic obstacle to understanding here.

A number of threads have now to be pulled together in the discussion. The task is most easily approached through a question that may be a source of residual unease about the argument of this chapter. It is the question of Marx's apparent reluctance to speak of ideology in connection with the proletariat and, in consequence, of the ideological significance of his own work. It can scarcely be doubted that this has been of considerable historical importance in preparing the ground for the propagation of the cognitive–defect theory, and it remains an obstacle to a clear view of the issues. If the case argued for here has acquired any solidity, the problem is one of rescuing some recalcitrant appearances. It should be noted that these are not nearly so one-sided as is often assumed. In the 1859 'Preface' ideology appears as the medium in which all sides fight out the social conflict, and the idea of 'proletarian ideology', if not the phrase itself, is manifestly present there. Moreover, the discussion in *The German Ideology* of the way large-scale industry destroyed for the proletarians 'their entire ideological superstructure' suffices to show that Marx did not suffer from any linguistic taboos in this area. But even when the significance of such references has been recognized, it remains the case that there is something to be saved. For they may well be felt to be unrepresentative of the main tendency of his usage. The need may be thought to emerge the more clearly if one compares the practice of Lenin and Lukács. Both are prepared to speak in the most frank and natural way of ideology in connection with the struggle of the proletariat, and indeed of Marxism itself as an ideology.[54] The explicitness of such references has generally been accepted as ruling out the possibility of any extension of the cognitive-defect thesis to either of them. Instead, it has been used to try to drive a wedge between their position and that of Marx, and so dismember the classical Marxist tradition.[55] This is an important misconception and needs to be dealt with by going to its source.

The comparison with Lenin and Lukács is a help in trying to focus on the specificity of Marx's situation. It serves to remind one of an aspect of it which has already been noted but whose importance is easily underplayed; the peculiarly combative and, one might say, negative character of his interest in the ideological. From this standpoint the failure to say much about the ideology of the proletariat presents no greater mystery than the failure to say much about ideology in general, and is due to the same cause. It is because he says so little about anything apart from the defects of particular forms of bourgeois ideology. The obsessional concern with unmasking the ruling ideas tends to appropriate the entire field of discourse. The few occasions on which his sights are set a little higher, as in the examples just given, bear out the assumption that there would be no theoretical difficulty in accommodating the phenomenon of proletarian ideology were the need to do so experienced in some more pressing way. In all this one has to allow something to the influence of individual preoccupations and intellectual styles. But there are other factors involved. The raising of sights was something to which Lenin and Lukács were impelled by virtue of their historical situation. Their task was not that of articulating a new world-view in opposition to existing tendencies, nor of establishing its credentials as against the products of bourgeois culture. Marx's achievement in these respects did not need to be repeated. It could largely be taken as given, and used as a basis for the continuing development that was necessary. In particular, there was the problem of how to equip the proletarian movement for the ideological struggle with the intellectual weapons he had created. This was the task to which they, in different ways, addressed themselves. In doing so, of course, the question of the positive character of proletarian ideology has to be moved right to the centre of the stage. Such a move is in no way contrary to the logic of the original position, but represents rather its natural development in different conditions and under the pressure of different concerns. Against this background the absence in Marx of a developed, selfconscious interest in the nature of proletarian ideology appears as an aspect of his general unconcern with the details of a theory of revolution. In consequence, his apprehension of the process through which class society is overthrown suffers from a lack of concreteness which had to be remedied by his successors. The verbal contrasts that reflect this development should not be allowed to obscure the basic continuities at work.

This is perhaps all that needs to be said to save the appearances. But much of the true significance of the problem would be missed if one were to be content with such a resolution of it. Marx's reluctance to deal explicitly with the concrete nature of proletarian ideology is not to be wholly ascribed to more or less contingent features of his position. Its sources go deeper and connect with issues of great importance for our argument. What still remain to be assimilated are the full implications of his conception of the proletariat and its role in history. That conception needs, in its turn, to be set against the larger theoretical background of the development of the class struggle as a whole and of its ideological forms. An important element in the background is the idea that, quite generally, rising classes put themselves forward as the representatives of society as a whole: ' . . . each new class which puts itself in the place of one ruling before it, is compelled, merely in order to carry through its aim, to present its interest as the common interest of all the members of society, that is, expressed in ideal form: it has to give its ideas the form of universality, and represent them as the only rational, universally valid ones'.[56] In the past, whenever the new class has achieved power these claims to universality have turned out to be a sham. It has proceeded to impose its rule on society while the conflict between classes goes on. The advent of the proletariat brings a new element to the situation. As *The Communist Manifesto* puts it:

> All previous historical movements were movements of minorities, or in the interest of minorities. The proletarian movement is the self-conscious independent movement of the immense majority, in the interest of the immense majority. The proletariat, the lowest stratum of our present society, cannot stir, cannot raise itself up, without the whole superincumbent strata of official society being sprung into the air.[57]

Thus, the proletariat alone is fitted to be the genuine 'universal representative', the sole instrument by which the class basis of society and with it the pre-history of mankind are abolished. Inherent in this situation is a strong element of dialectical tension. The proletariat has to be perceived both as a class and as the negation of class society. Marx's language reflects the strain of rendering such a perception accurately. It shows itself characteristically in the resort to paradox: the proletariat is 'a class of civil society which is not a class of civil society, a class which is the dissolution of all classes',[58] 'the class which no longer counts as a class in society, is not recognized as a class, and is in itself the expression of the dissolution of all classes, nationalities, etc., within present society'.[59] It is clear that there must be some difficulty about attributing class interests in the ordinary way to such an entity. Its interests are not to be seen as partial and specific to itself, but are rather to be identified with those of humanity in general. It is a sphere of society which 'can . . . redeem itself only through the *total redemption of humanity*',[60] and 'the emancipation of the workers contains universal human emancipation'.[61] The difficulty about the attribution of interests is explicitly recognized by Marx as an expression of the conditions that must be fulfilled if the proletariat is to carry out its historical task:

> This subsuming of individuals under definite classes cannot be abolished until a class has taken shape, which has no longer any particular class interest to assert against the ruling class.[62]

In the light of the conceptual nexus which has been the main concern of this essay, it is not surprising that the difficulty of attribution should have repercussions for ideology also. The ideology of a class is the set of representations that serve its particular interests. No problems arise in speaking of the ideology of previous ruling classes since their claims to represent anything other than such interests are spurious. But the interests of the proletariat are genuinely universal, and their complete realization implies the end of all ideology. Marx's response to this situation is perhaps most adequately rendered by noting the dual perspective it enjoins on him. For many purposes he is content to treat the proletariat as one class among others, subject to the ordinary dynamics of the class struggle and amenable to the general mode of analysis appropriate to that struggle. Alongside this must be placed his awareness of all that sets it apart, its status as the expression of the dissolution of classes, and the temptation that results to regard it as already virtually identical with the human community of the post-revolutionary world. Thus, there are occasions when he sees it in ways appropriate to its role as the beneficiary of a particular ideology. This is the element in his position that was to be so strikingly developed by Lenin and Lukács. But there is also the tendency to view it as the enemy and destroyer of ideology in general. That tendency corresponds to the deepest level of his thinking: the sense of the uniqueness of its destiny is close to the heart of the system as a whole. In his practice of ideological analysis it is allowed to operate with particular freedom and purity. What is reflected there is scarcely at all the proletariat as a class struggling with other classes in and through ideology, but instead the proletariat as the harbinger and begetter of new, non-ideological forms of con-sciousness. Thus there is, one might say, a deep-seated antipathy between the context in which it is natural to speak of ideology and the context in which Marx's hopes for the proletariat find fullest expression. In the complex tensions generated by this antipathy lies the secret of the linguistic pattern we have been seeking to explain.

The special character of proletarian consciousness holds the key to yet greater mysteries. Attention has already been drawn to the significance in Marx, Lenin and Lukács of the image of a unified structure of consciousness centred on the proletariat and incorporating the true and the spontaneous together with ideology. It was noted that our presentation was as yet incomplete. In particular, it omitted the part played by the scientific understanding of society. It is time to repair this, and to redeem the undertaking to draw together the themes of ideology, class consciousness and social science so as to reveal the unity of Marx's thought. Such a redemption can be achieved here only in a programmatic sort of way. The connections involved need to be worked out at a variety of levels and in a mass of concrete detail to do justice to the richness of the subject. Ideology is the only element which has been treated in this essay on anything like the scale required for such a task. Nevertheless, it should be possible to take advantage of its strategic significance, its ramified links with the other factors, sufficiently to exhibit at least the skeleton of the structure as a whole. As one might expect, Marx's failure to provide much direct help in giving an account of the individual parts is repeated with emphasis when it comes to the question of their systematic interconnection. Again one has to rely on the unity of vision that is immanent in the particulars and will reveal itself if they are approached in the right way. There is an additional source of guidance which it should now be possible to exploit. It consists of the contributions of those who have had the deepest grasp of the distinctive coherence of his thought and have done most to give it expression. Here again we shall find the work of Lenin and Lukács making a special claim on our attention. At this level also, where the issue concerns the structure of the forms of social consciousness in general, one has to recognize their organic and rigorous development of the original impulse, and once more we find ourselves in contact with a unified tradition of thought.

It may be well to acknowledge at once that when the factor of scientific understanding is introduced into the picture, epistemological questions can scarcely be avoided. For, of course, questions of this kind do arise in connection with Marx's work, and they are not conjured out of existence just by coming to realize that in it ideology is not an epistemological category. That insight is rather a necessary preliminary for tackling them in a fruitful way. It disposes of the temptation to try to discuss them in a systematically-misleading idiom, and this is itself a significant part of the benefits of getting clear about ideology. An obvious point at which such questions arise is in connection with the status of the spontaneous consciousness of the proletariat. Marx is quite certainly committed to claiming some measure of cognitive superiority for it, over that of other classes. The tendency, as Lukács points out, is to be found as early in his career as the remarks on the Weavers' Uprising in Silesia, and it remains a characteristic element thereafter.[63] Towards the end of his life it finds another kind of expression in the preface to the *Enquête Ouvrière* where the workers are exhorted to reply to the questionnaire, since only they can describe 'with full knowledge the evils which they endure'.[64] Variations on the theme occur with great frequency in the intervening years in such passages as the following:

For the proletarians . . . the conditions of their existence, labour, and with it all the conditions of existence governing modern society, have become something accidental, something over which they, as separate individuals, have no control, and over which no *social* organisation can give them control. The contradiction between the individuality of each separate proletarian and labour, the condition of life forced upon him, becomes evident to him himself, for he is sacrificed from youth upwards and, within his own class, has no chance of arriving at the conditions which would place him in the other class.[65]

As these examples suggest, the basic idea behind the optimism is straightforward enough. There are some things which only the workers can know and which 'become evident' to them on the basis of their life experience: they have, in the hackneyed expression, the truth of these matters in their bones. The proletariat is, by virtue of its location in the mode of production, in a privileged position in certain respects. From that location unfolds a perspective which enforces an awareness of some basic social realities, and this awareness is of great epistemological significance. The process by which the proletariat is impelled beyond the phenomenal forms of bourgeois society has an analogue in the scientific enterprise itself, in so far as that too involves the penetration of appearances to the reality behind. This is not to be taken merely as a suggestive metaphor. The point is rather that the sense of its situation naturally available to the proletariat contains in embryo the possibility of a scientific account of society. The central scientific concepts may be seen as refinements of insights characteristic, in the first place, of spontaneous proletarian consciousness. It is necessary to be specific here. What the proletariat is made aware of by virtue of its life experience are such realities as the existence of social classes, of conflicting class interests, of exploitation and of its own status as a commodity. The concept of class struggle is perhaps the most obvious scientific precipitate of these insights. But the same relationship holds between the workers' awareness of exploitation and the concept of surplus value, and between their awareness of their role in the market and the concept of labour power. With these concepts is unlocked the entire scheme of the Marxist analysis of capitalist society. Thus, it may now be said that spontaneous proletarian consciousness provides the basis for science just in the sense that a rational reconstruction of a scientific account of society could be given which would exhibit its insights as the starting point. It is in this way that one should understand the familiar claim that the science of society is based upon or presupposes the class standpoint of the proletariat.

It is once again important here to bear in mind the theoretical background of Marx's conception. The claims made for the proletariat are not the expression of an irrational fixation, but the culmination of a line of reasoning which has a general relevance. He is well aware that the bourgeoisie too, in its heroic period, had special access to truths about the society it was seeking to dominate. A recognition of the positive achievements of bourgeois thought and, hence, an opposition to apocalyptic views of those of the proletariat, are a marked feature of the tradition we are considering. Lenin justifies his position on the issue by pointing out that 'Marx based his work on the firm foundation of the human knowledge acquired under capitalism', and that he achieved his results by 'fully assimilating all that earlier science had produced'.[66] Lukács insists that 'proletarian thought does not require a *tabula rasa*, a new start to the task of comprehending reality and one without any preconceptions', but rather 'conceives of bourgeois society together with its intellectual and artistic productions as the *point of departure* for its own method'.[67] It is common ground to these thinkers that the class position of the rising bourgeoisie permitted it insights which formed the basis for valuable theoretical work. As one might expect of a class struggling to assert itself, they included a grasp of the reality of class conflict. Marx declares flatly that he deserves no credit 'for discovering the existence of classes in modern society or the struggle between them'. 'Long before me', he explains, 'bourgeois historians had described the historical development of this class struggle and bourgeois economists the economic anatomy of the classes.'[68] It is also clear that the resources of bourgeois thought extend to at least a partial grasp of the notion of surplus value. Marx draws attention on many occasions to its active presence in the writings of Smith and Ricardo, though acknowledging that it is never raised there to the level of an adequate theoretical formulation. These writers are unable to escape from the form it takes in capitalist society so as to investigate the general category: 'All economists share the error of examining surplus-value not as such, in its pure form, but in the particular forms of profit and rent.'[69] Moreover, their perspective is permanently confined within the controlling ideological assumption:

> Ricardo never concerns himself about the origin of surplus-value. He treats it as a thing inherent in the capitalist mode of production, which mode, in his eyes, is the natural form of social production.[70]

A grasp of the true nature of labour as a commodity is still further removed from the bourgeois purview. The difficulties into which the classical theory of value had fallen had to await a clear statement of the distinction between labour and labour power. In this area at least, Marx is inclined to make claims for his own originality. In connection with the dual character of labour as a creator of use-values and as itself the possessor of exchange-value, he remarks: 'I was the first to point out and to examine critically this two-fold nature of the labour contained in commodities', and adds that 'this point is the pivot on which a clear comprehension of Political Economy turns'.[71] It is so, in so far as it constitutes the vital clue to the nature of the commodity structure as a whole. The complete theoretical comprehension of that structure falls outside the scope of classical political economy, and here one is again brought up against the objective limits of bourgeois thought. What needs to be emphasized for present purposes, however, is that these limits leave room for substantial achievements which are internally related to insights available in the spontaneous consciousness of the bourgeoisie while it was still a progressive force in history. They are, of course, insights available also to the proletariat: in so far as the standpoints of the two classes constitute a basis for science they may be regarded as having, as it were, the same co-ordinates. The intellectual achievements of the classical political economists are explicable as a theoretical articulation of this common starting point. It is important to bear this in mind in considering the notion of 'proletarian science'. The proletariat is not the ultimate repository of science through some magical intervention in history, but through the secular process of its unfolding. It is in the logic of that process that one must ground the claim that it alone can achieve a comprehensive view of social reality, free of the contradictions that beset other classes. It is also in terms of that logic that the precarious nature of the bourgeois achievement should be understood. Marx, as has already been noted, displays an acute sense of the chronology involved.[72] When the bourgeoisie has established its dominance and, more especially, when it begins to experience significant pressure from below, a gradual transformation affects all aspects of its thought. The spontaneous drift of its consciousness becomes set towards the mystification of social arrangements, even towards the elimination of its own previous insights through the development of notions of a just wage, of a natural harmony of interests in society and so on. The refinement of such notions at the level of social theory can produce only a systematizing of myth. Thus sets in that general intellectual decline diagnosed by Marx through such representative figures as the utilitarian philosophers and the vulgar economists. What it signifies is that the bourgeois standpoint is no longer available as a basis for science, and that the responsibility for further progress has passed entirely to the proletariat.

The discussion here has been concerned with discovering in what sense one may speak of the integration of scientific work with the empirical consciousness of the proletariat. The actual achievement of this result is, it must be remembered, itself an historical event which occurs as part of a fundamental process of change leading to the creation of a new kind of society. This historical process is the indispensable background against which a demonstration of the unity of Marx's thought has to be situated. In terms of it the remaining elements of the picture may now be sketched in rapidly. A central feature of the process is the development of the empirically-given consciousness of the proletariat into true class consciousness. This is 'the sense, become conscious, of the historical role of the class',[73] involving an awareness on the part of the workers of 'the irreconcilable antagonism of their interests to the whole of the modern political and social system'.[74] Such awareness clearly rests upon a substantial cognitive achievement, a developed understanding of the nature of the modern system and of the place of the class within it. That is, it presupposes the diffusion within the proletariat of a considerable measure of scientific insight.

It now begins to be clear how ideology fits into the picture. The ideology of the proletariat, as has been seen, only comes into existence as an expression of authentic class consciousness: whatever falls short of that must be accounted among the resources of the ruling class.[75] Hence it follows that it has to arise on the basis of scientific achievement. To note this dependence is to be made aware of another aspect of the relationship between science and the standpoint of the proletariat, and specifically the standpoint of its class interests. All class ideologies are, of necessity, involved in claims to knowledge about society. What distinguishes the ideology of the proletariat is that in its case the cognitive content is supplied by science: 'it is this that gives the class struggle of the proletariat its special place among other class struggles, namely that it obtains its sharpest weapons from the hand of true science, from its clear insight into reality'.[76] This idea that science and ideology come together in the historical reality of the proletariat is a central theme of the tradition we are dealing with, and is what ultimately sustains the spirit of rational optimism that is so pervasive a feature of it. In the case of the proletariat alone the pursuit of truth and the demands of historical existence are found in a state not simply of compatibility but of reciprocal dependence. This relationship is significant in a number of important ways. It is in virtue of it that the proletariat can intelligibly be regarded both as a class and as the representative of humanity. Moreover, it creates the possibility for it to rehearse in its own existence the conditions of the post-revolutionary society, and so establish a concrete basis for a rational belief in their viability. For present purposes what has to be particularly noted is that the coming together of ideology and science enables one to add the final element to the skeleton contracted for earlier. There has now emerged a picture of the empirical and the true con-sciousness of the proletariat grown together on the basis of scientific work and issuing in the ideological weapons with which the historical struggle is conducted. At this point the vision of a unified structure centred on the proletariat is in all essentials complete.

The unity involved here is the unity of a structure of consciousness. Yet it is not to be realised through reflection alone, nor through any set of operations confined to the realm of thought. It comes into existence as an historical reality through a many-sided process of struggle. This is the direction in which Marxist philosophy always bids us look: 'All mysteries which lead theory to mysticism find their rational solution in human praxis and in the comprehension of this praxis.'[77] The idea that the solution of theoretical problems might have to be found in and through praxis was not plucked by Marx from the air. Here, as elsewhere, he was building on the firm foundation of existing human knowledge, and specifically on the achievements of classical German philosophy. The definitive account from within Marxism of the relationships involved has been given by Lukács. In the course of it, he points out that Kant had attempted in the *Critique of Practical Reason* 'to show that the barriers that could not be overcome by theory (contemplation) were amenable to practical solutions', and that Fichte had gone beyond this and 'put the practical, action and activity in the centre of his unifying philosophical system'.[78] The vital turn towards history, as the arena in which the practical assumes its true significance for thought was also taken in classical philosophy. But with this move, as Lukács shows, it reached the limits of its success. It was unable to apprehend the concrete character of that specific form of historical praxis that alone is decisive for the solution of its problems. For the subject and agent of this praxis is the proletariat, and an adequate depiction of its role is impossible from the purely bourgeois point of view. At this point, 'classical philosophy turned back and lost itself in the endless labyrinth of conceptual mythology'.[79] It was Hegel, 'in every respect the pinnacle of this development', who also 'made the most strenuous search for this subject'.[80] The device of the World Spirit only succeeds, however, in giving the problems a transcendental gloss, taking them out of the realm of human history in which alone their solution is to be found. Thus, classical philosophy reaches the point at which the path ahead is clearly visible but is itself unable to make any progress along it. Now, however, another aspect of its achievement becomes crucial. This is its success in fashioning the indispensable instrument of such further progress, the dialectical method. It is not an accident that the tradition of thought which grasped the theoretical significance of praxis should also have laid the foundations of the dialectic. This significance is, as the history of positivism and empiricism shows, invisible to non-dialectical thought. On the othe hand, an

understanding of the conditions for the successful application of the method leads one naturally to the sphere of
human action. For this constitutes the basic paradigm of the
medium that is required. As a form of mediation between
ideas and the world it gives substance to the possibility that
attributes of each may come together in a concrete fashion.
Above all, its dual aspect serves to suggest how the
fundamental requirement might be met, that the dialectical
categories should retain their logical character while yet
applying to reality. It remains to find the subject in whose
mode of operation this possibility is fully realized. The tragic
quality of the classical German tradition derives from the
fact that the class which is the discoverer of the method is
unable to constitute itself as such a subject. The bourgeoisie
is precluded from this by the limitations and contradictions
of its consciousness which in turn reflect the nature of its
objective situation. Instead the achievement is reserved for
the class which was able to find 'within itself on the basis of
its life-experience' the subject of action, namely the
proletariat.[81]

It is along such lines as these that one must explicate the
thesis that the historical role of the proletariat is of decisive
significance for philosophy. That thesis has a central place in
the thought of the major figures we have been discussing.
The claim by Engels that the German working-class
movement is the heir of German classical philosophy may
stand for a commitment shared by all of them. None held it
with a more spectacular emphasis than did Lukács. *History
and Class Consciousness* may be seen, in large part, as an
attempt to fill out the significance of Engels's remark and
demonstrate its correctness. Reference was made in the
previous chapter to the scale of the metaphysical ambitions
for the proletariat that the attempt involved.[82] It may be
worthwhile to look at this issue again in the light of the
intervening discussion, and particularly at the suggestion
that the theme mythologized in the work is, in itself, an
essential ingredient in Marxist thought. The discussion may

have served to increase one's sympathy with Lukács's
ambitions by showing the extent to which they can claim a
legitimate basis. They embody hopes that are inextricably
bound up with the programme of Marxist philosophy, and, in
particular, with the conception of its dialectic. When seen
against this background, the unity of theory and practice in
the proletariat must indeed be recognized as having
implications for traditional problems of philosophy. Thus, to
stay within the terms of his discussion, it has such
implications for what he takes to be the vital question of 'the
irrational', the senseless substratum that lies outside the
reach of reason, the amorphous content that resists all
imposition of form, the being that is the ineluctable 'other' of
consciousness. Proletarian praxis, by managing, as it were,
to suffuse a particular segment of reality with thought, places
the general problem of redeeming this inert material in a new
light. In doing so it enables one to see how the antinomies
discussed by Lukács, of form and content and of being and
consciousness, might become amenable to treatment. Thus,
a successful account of the Marxist dialectic might be
expected to show how, in the context of human history,
some familiar ontological and epistemological issues can
assume more tractable forms. This is, however, not
achieved in *History and Class Consciousness*. The explanation of the failure takes one back to the weakness, as later
diagnosed by Lukács himself, in the 'central concept' of
praxis; the 'abstract and idealistic' character it assumes by
being interpreted solely in terms of a struggle for consciousness. Hence it is that the identical subject-object of
history turns out to be 'a purely metaphysical construct'.
The question of whether 'a genuinely identical subject-
object' can 'be created by self-knowledge, however
adequate, and however truly based on an adequate
knowledge of society' has, he suggests, only to be
formulated precisely 'to see that it must be answered in the
negative'.[83] But if the identical subject-object has not been
found, the rest of the structure collapses and he has failed to

establish his interpretation of Engels's dictum. The anti-
nomy of subject and object is basic in the scheme,[84] and
unless it is resolved there is, as it were, no substance in
which the elements of the others can cohere. This failure
lends additional point to the familiar charge of idealism. It
stems, one might now say, from a systematic inability to do
justice to one side of the dialectical story; the side of being,
content, the object. The dialectic of consciousness is not
rich enough to accommodate the specificity of these factors:
for its purposes they have to be either ignored or completely
assimilated into the subjective. Such a dialectic may succeed
in moving with unparalleled ease and precision in its own
sphere. But the atmosphere in which it thrives is too thin to
support the actual density and refractoriness of the objective
processes of history. Hence, the idealist drive towards the
breaking down of all differentiation, towards the ultimate
simplicity of the object of thought, must prove too strong for
Lukács's chances of carrying out the Marxist programme.

The drive shows itself in a great variety of ways in *History
and Class Consciousness*. It does so in the series of
reductions and identities that characterizes the main
intellectual structure of the work. The idea that the 'reform
of consciousness' simply is 'the revolutionary process
itself'[85] is the central case. But the tendency is also present
in the general treatment of the relations between the
categories of science, ideology and class consciousness. The
way in which ideological maturity is spoken of as though it
were actually identical with class consciousness has already
been noted.[86] Elsewhere there are formulations that suggest
that scientific understanding might be introduced as a third
element in the equation, as when we are reminded of the
importance of the question of how much the proletariat has
to suffer 'before it achieves ideological maturity, before it
acquires a true understanding of its class situation and a true
class consciousness'.[87] In all this, the intensity of Lukács's
feeling for the unity of Marx's vision is strikingly evident.
But his unresolved Hegelianism makes it impossible to

render it adequately: it emerges as mere conflation, a fake simplicity from which all shades of discrimination have been eliminated. To do justice to Marx's perception one has to retain a more active sense of complexity, a sense that the categories serve at least to theorize different aspects of the unity of proletarian consciousness. For this one needs a language that allows the recognition of types of logical affinity other than sheer identity, of more complex relationships of implication and presupposition.

To see these requirements satisfied, one may turn to the precise and concrete analyses of Lenin, a thinker who has an equally vivid conviction of unity but is free from the idealist strain in the rendering of it. They are fully embodied in, for instance, the awareness of the intricate pattern of relationships between the levels of social consciousness that pervades the argument of *What is to be Done?* Elsewhere this awareness is still more explicitly spelt out:

> . . . socialism, as the ideology of the class struggle of the proletariat, is subject to the general conditions governing the inception, development and consolidation of an ideology; in other words, it is founded on the sum-total of human knowledge, presupposes a high level of scientific development, demands scientific work, etc. etc. Socialism is *introduced* by the ideologists into the proletarian class struggle which develops spontaneously on the basis of capitalist relationships.[88]

In this passage all our major themes are restated and brought together; the foundation of socialist ideology on the sum-total of human knowledge, the presupposition by it of a high level of scientific development, and the need to weld it consciously together with the spontaneously given. It captures the true character of the relationships between the levels of spontaneity, ideology and science, and, above all, reminds us of the class struggle as the medium in which praxis achieves that articulation of all three that is the central propelling image of Marxist thought.

CHAPTER 4

TRADITIONS IN MARXISM

THIS essay began with an attempt to state the essentials of Marx's conception of ideology. It was argued that they are best captured in the formula that ideology is thought which serves class interests. The same idea was found to be central in the work of Lenin and Lukács, and was there developed and applied in ways that justify speaking of a single, evolving tradition. It is one which, in view of its membership, may reasonably be accorded a classic status within Marxist treatments of the subject. The formula was proposed as having the merit of fixing the notion in its place within the theory of class struggle. It can stand for the recognition that sets of ideas have ideological significance only in so far as they bring values to bear on the institutions and practices that are the site and the instruments of that struggle. The classic texts were drawn on to develop some models in terms of which this process may be understood. They served to suggest a distinction between a mode of operation that is 'semantic' in character and one that is 'syntactic', between cases where what is ideological is part of the meaning of particular elements and cases where it shows itself in their configuration and is enforced by formal analogy with the structures of the social world. The discussion was conducted against the background of a contrast between the classical position and some others that also lie under the umbrella of 'Marxism'. The contrast has an obvious chronological aspect: the alternatives were worked out after the close of Lenin's active career and the publication of *History and Class Consciousness* (1923).

There are two distinct directions in which one must look in

the later period, towards philosophy on the one hand and towards the theory of society on the other. In philosophy the significance of the notion of ideology has been primarily epistemological. It has been used to theorize certain cognitive states which have the social world as their object, but fail in one way or another to apprehend its true character. A typical expression of this tendency is the reliance on a dichotomy of 'the ideological' and 'the scientific'. In social theory ideology has come to serve as the focal point for a number of problems. It has been used to raise general questions about the social determination of ideas, about the nature of class consciousness, and about the sources of the cohesion of human societies. Taken together, the two directions of development involve a considerable modification and expansion of the original concept and its release from the specific context on which its sense depended. They can derive so little inspiration or support from the classical position that one is forced to recognize a serious discontinuity here. The impression of an organic connection can be sustained only through the systematic misreading of key texts, backed by the practice of assertion on a large scale. The consequence of all this is a considerable region of theoretical confusion and nullity in recent Marxist treatments of the subject. In pointing to it one has also to recognize the strength of the pressures that have brought it about. It would be extraordinary if the way in which the concept of ideology has changed were an accidental or isolated phenomenon. It is natural to look instead for some larger pattern in the development of Marxist thought into which it may be fitted. An appropriate one seems recently to have been provided ready-made in Perry Anderson's *Considerations on Western Marxism*.[1] Its attractions are such that one may be tempted to say at once that the post-classical history of the concept in the realms of philosophy and social theory simply is the unfolding of its destiny within 'Western Marxism'. The thesis of this essay would benefit if such a suggestion could be sustained, and, incidentally, Anderson's scheme of explanation should gain in substance and authority through being applied successfully in an important particular case. Before any of these advantages can be reaped, however, there is an irksome difficulty to be overcome. The process of doing so will shed some light both on the strengths and weaknesses of his scheme and on the general interpretation of our thesis.

The difficulty is that while *History and Class Consciousness* has been depicted here as a major text of the classical tradition, Anderson locates it firmly within the 'Western Marxism' of which Lukács is taken to be a representative figure. His initial approach to the distinction is made through certain 'generational and geographical' criteria. Lukács does not fit them neatly, having been born earlier, and further east, than some members of the classical group. These, however, could only be minor anomalies, and in any case, the criteria themselves represent merely a first approximation to the theme:

> The historical dates and geographical distribution of 'Western Marxism' provide the preliminary formal framework for situating it within the evolution of socialist thought as a whole. It remains to identify the specific substantive traits which define and demarcate it as an integrated tradition.[2]

It is when one comes to consider these 'specific traits' that serious misgivings arise. The 'first and most fundamental' of them 'has been the structural divorce of this Marxism from political practice'.[3] This scarcely seems an apt description of the situation of the younger Lukács who, as Anderson notes, was a Deputy People's Commissar in the Hungarian Soviet Republic, fought with its revolutionary army, and played a leading role in the Hungarian Communist Party in the twenties, briefly becoming its general secretary in 1928.[4] It was only from 1929 onwards that he 'ceased to be a political militant, confining himself to literary criticism and philosophy in his intellectual work'.[5] A second defining feature of the tradition which seems hardly more appropriate

to his case is its 'consistent pessimism': 'The hidden
hallmark of Western Marxism as a whole is . . . that it is a
product of *defeat*'.[6] 'Its major works', Anderson asserts,
'were, without exception, produced in situations of political
isolation and despair', and he goes on at once in illustration
of this: 'Lukács's *History and Class Consciousness* (1923)
was written in exile in Vienna, while white terror raged in
Hungry after the supression of the Hungarian Commune.'[7]
Even as a thumbnail sketch this is highly tendentious.
Lukács's own testimony strongly suggests that he was
suffering at the time neither from isolation nor despair. On
the contrary:

> As a member of the inner collective of *Communism* I was active in
> helping to work out a new 'left-wing' political and theoretical line.
> It was based on the belief, very much alive at the time, that the great
> revolutionary wave that would soon sweep the whole world, or
> Europe at the very least, to socialism, had in no way been broken by
> the setbacks in Finland, Hungary and Munich. Events like the
> Kapp Putsch, the occupation of the factories in Italy, the
> Polish-Soviet War and even the March Action, strengthened our
> belief in the imminence of world revolution and the total
> transformation of the civilised world.[8]

There seems no good reason for doubting this account: it has
been generally accepted by people who knew him well and
by later scholars.[9] Moreover, the internal evidence of the
text itself is unequivocal and, surely, decisive. Pessimism is
almost the last attribute one would naturally associate with
it, and indeed its characteristic defects stem rather, as we
have seen, from a surfeit of the opposite.[10] It seems
reasonable to suggest at this point that some adjustment
needs to be made in Anderson's scheme.

An obvious possibility, which is supported by many of the
details of his discussion, is that one's sense of the
chronology needs to be revised. That is to say, the critical
time for the origins of 'Western Marxism' should be shifted
deeper into the interwar period, clearly postdating *History
and Class Consciousness*. This looks like a step in the right

direction. It would, however, be a mistake to suppose that it could be taken without affecting the rest of the analysis. The discussion of Lukács's case has methodological implications also: in particular it sheds an unfavourable light on Anderson's tendency to rely on lists of major figures to enforce the distinctions he requires.[11] This leaves the impression that the primary unit of the scheme is the individual 'career', treated as a homogeneous entity. Taken together a cluster of contemporaneous careers forms a 'generation', and two or more generations are apt to be considered a 'tradition'. The result, in a curious echo of old-fashioned styles of bourgeois historiography, is a somewhat rigid and unwieldy framework that seems ill-suited to coping with the fluidity of historical process and movement. It must tend to abstract from the significance of those events in the public realm that are always liable to cut across the careers of individuals; disrupting, reshaping, crowning or untimely terminating them, and creating as they do so new patterns of continuity and discontinuity within and across generations. It is not difficult, at least at the level of explanation that concerns us here, to see what are the developments of this kind that shape the emergence of post-classical Marxism. Anderson draws attention to them again and again: in this respect his narrative is better than, and works against, his taxonomy. The general background is constituted by 'the failure of proletarian revolutions in the advanced zones of European capitalism after the First World War'.[12] The rise of Fascism and Stalinism are the specific mediations that are decisive for our theme. Their significance is illustrated in the way Lukács was forced out of active party politics by growing Stalinist pressures in the late twenties, and then into exile in the Soviet Union by the Nazi victory in Germany. It emerges also in Anderson's account of how the members of the Frankfurt Institute, the quintessential 'Western Marxists', were driven by the same circumstances into exile in the opposite direction and into an ever deepening retreat from active politics.[13] His feeling for the essentials of the story is further shown when going beyond the more formal attributes of the tradition to characterize its distinctive preoccupations and subject matter. The first point to be noted is 'a basic shift in the whole centre of gravity of European Marxism towards *philosophy*'[14] and, specifically, 'a marked predominance of epistemological work'.[15] When 'Western Marxism' did proceed 'beyond questions of method to matters of substance' it 'came to concentrate overwhelmingly on study of *superstructures*'.[16] Here too the influence of the basic determinants is made quite clear:

> In the absence of the magnetic pole of a revolutionary class movement, the needle of the whole tradition tended to swing increasingly away towards contemporary bourgeois culture. The original relationship between Marxist theory and proletarian practice was subtly but steadily substituted by a new relationship between Marxist theory and bourgeois theory.[17]

Hence it is that one encounters

> the studied silence of Western Marxism in those areas most central to the classical traditions of historical materialism: scrutiny of the economic laws of motion of capitalism as a mode of production, analysis of the political machinery of the bourgeois state, strategy of the class struggle necessary to overthrow it.[18]

Gramsci is, as Anderson remarks, 'the single exception to this rule',[19] the last Western Marxist thinker 'to broach central issues of class struggle directly in his writings'.[20] This point will have to be taken up later. For the present we may simply note that the circle of traits defining 'Western Marxism' is now complete: it is comprised of a remoteness from political practice, a pervasive pessimism, and a theoretical concentration on epistemological and super-structural questions.

The ease with which the case of ideology fits into this account hardly needs, in the light of the preceding discussion, to be expatiated on at length. The disengagement from the theory of class struggle described by Anderson left the notion free to embark on a fresh career, and the pressure of the new interests he cites ensured that it would do so. When Marxist thinkers became preoccupied with questions of epistemology and with theorizing the superstructure of bourgeois society, it was natural that they should turn for help in devising the necessary tools of inquiry to the classical writers, and especially to Marx. As he had never had the opportunity to develop a sustained interest in either field, it was a meagre inheritance on which to draw. Among the small stock of concepts with some semblance of eligibility, ideology had a prominent place. Obviously, it had in Marx's usage something 'superstructural' about it. When this sense is reified and drained of its specificity the concept becomes available for new tasks, to theorize a formation of the superstructure or the place within it of consciousness in general. Moreover, as our discussion has shown, circumstances combined to give the original idea other kinds of potential. The failure to register the real significance of Marx's interest in ideological error, together with a fetishized use of Engels's remarks about 'false consciousness', provided the impetus needed to transform it into a category of epistemology. These developments, as Anderson's account would suggest, occur in the context of a growing interaction with bourgeois theory. In that sphere, once the concept had been assimilated, the dominance of sociological and epistemological themes was wholly to be expected, not least in view of their usefulness for drawing the teeth of the original Marxist doctrine.[21] Thus it was that the concept of ideology came to acquire the theoretical burdens with which this essay has been concerned. As Anderson's discussion would also lead one to expect, they have not been cheerfully borne. The pessimism of which he speaks is as marked here as elsewhere, finding perhaps its most developed expression in Althusser's insistence that even a communist society cannot escape the imaginary, distorted, ideological relationship.[22]

It seems fair to conclude that *Considerations on Western*

Marxism offers many important elements of the framework of historical understanding our theme requires. It should be added, however, that, even at the level of a preliminary conceptualization, the actual framework it contains is in need of some theoretical modification and enrichment. The need arises in large part from a curious feature of the work, the extent of its 'studied silence' on the question of the dialectic. The few references to it are entirely casual, and simply represent enforced acknowledgements of the concerns of the subjects of the discussion.[23] Such a treatment altogether fails to do justice to the significance it had for most of these thinkers. For the rest the silence is complete, even where its effect is unnatural, as in the attempts to draw up the unfinished agenda of Marxist thought.[24] The suspicion that it reflects the fact that the question does not loom very large in Anderson's view of things is, unfortunately, supported by his methodology. The barren and ossified character of the taxonomy is again significant here. A dialectical approach must surely sweep away the schematism of careers and generations, so as to allow the shape of the conceptual field to reflect directly the fate of the socialist movement within the totality of the historical process. The dangers of hypostatized categories need no further emphasis in this essay so far as ideology is concerned.[25] It has been shown that the tendency is a characteristic weakness of the post-classical literature on the subject. But the dialectic is not simply involved here as a source of reminders of the need to preserve fluid categories. The discussion has also noted a familiar sense in which the specifically dialectical quality of the concept of ideology has to be borne in mind. This sense arises from its role in theorizing the dynamic processes of conflict and contradiction that constitute the class struggle in the realm of ideas. It is a role which has to be grasped in a spirit different from that of Anderson's approach and, indeed, it is only within a dialectical perspective that his specific insights can be made to yield their full significance.

These issues may be taken a stage further by looking more

closely at a particularly interesting and ambiguous figure in his account. The recognition that Gramsci took no part in the retreat from the theory of class struggle has already been noted, and his position is anomalous in other ways also. He was 'the one major theorist in the West who was not a philosopher but a politician'.[26] Moreover, his case 'symbolizes, in its very exception, the historical rule that governed (the) general retreat of theory from classical Marxist parlance',[27] and, unlike the other major representatives of 'Western Marxism', 'the primary object of his theoretical enquiry was not the realm of art'.[28] The scale of these qualifications is enough to suggest that in a more flexible scheme he would be accepted as a transitional or intermediary figure, rather than assigned to a category to most of whose constituting rules he is an exception. Such an acceptance would allow recognition of the genuine affinities he does possess with 'Western Marxism'. Thus, his personal fate illustrates, in the most dramatic way, the impact of Fascism on the working-class movement. His intellectual work was 'unremittingly centred on superstructural objects', and achievement in this field is usually taken to be the chief source of his importance as a theorist. It is true, however, that, as Anderson goes on to point out, the field was treated by him in a distinctive way: 'unlike any other theorist in Western Marxism he took the autonomy and efficacy of cultural superstructures as a *political* problem, to be explicitly theorized as such – in its relationship to the maintenance or subversion of the social order'.[29] To say this is just to acknowledge once more the central fact of his continued commitment to issues of class struggle. The point that is now emerging is the conventional one that his achievement lay in pursuing the theoretical implications of these issues into areas untouched by Marx or Lenin, but which are vital for revolutionary strategy in advanced capitalist societies. In accepting it, there is another complication to be borne in mind, one that testifies again to the way he straddles the two worlds of Marxism. For his case is not simply one of the extension or novel application of classical themes. They now appear bathed, as it were, in a different light: everything falls under the rubric to which he was so partial of 'pessimism of the intellect, optimism of the will'.[30] However this is glossed, it could not naturally serve to encapsulate the views of Marx or Lenin. They had their moments of personal doubt, or even despair, but their characteristic doctrine can only properly be described as one of an optimism of the intellect and of the will: its central thrust is always towards the laying of rational foundations for the goal of the socialist society. Gramsci's slogan signifies the beginnings of the transformation of this position into a species of stoicism, a process that was to establish the characteristic tone of voice of 'Western Marxism' as a whole. The stance it expresses is an honourable and, in some ways, an attractive one, but it is not that of the classical writers.

The scattered references to ideology in the *Prison Notebooks* bear the marks of this complex background. The reader is, for much of the time, in a familiar world, borne along by the pressure of an obvious and vivid concern with questions of class struggle, and reassured by the standard imagery of 'ideological weapons' and 'the ideological front'.[31] Much of what is usually regarded as Gramsci's distinctive theoretical contribution poses no special problem either. Thus, the difficult notion of 'hegemony' may be taken as embodying, among other things, a recognition of the pervasive character of bourgeois ideology, and the need to combat it at a multiplicity of levels. As such it represents a theoretical refinement of insights which, as was remarked earlier, are already present in Marx's writings on contemporary history.[32] As against all this, however, one has to set the influence of the specifically 'Western Marxist' dimension of the text. It shows itself in the first place in the familiar shape of a tendency towards conceptual inflation and reification. Here, for instance, one should note the conception of the way in which ideology 'serves to cement and to unify' an 'entire social bloc'.[33] The image of ideology as social cement was to be found deeply congenial in later Marxism, and an instance of its use has been noted in discussing the work of Poulantzas.[34] Still more interesting, however, is the way in which the dual character of the new concerns is reflected in Gramsci's argument. It is caught, for instance, in the comment, on the 1859 'Preface', that 'the thesis which asserts that men become conscious of fundamental conflicts on the level of ideology is not psychological or moralistic in character, but structural and epistemological'.[35] The claim that the significance of ideology is structural and epistemological could hardly be improved on as a statement of what is distinctive in the post-classical treatment of the subject. But here one must again heed his own warning against reading too much into 'single casual affirmations and isolated aphorisms'. A solider significance may be attached to his more extended discussion of the development of usage in this area. Gramsci remarks that 'the meaning which the term "ideology" has assumed in Marxist philosophy implicitly contains a negative value judgement'. He goes on to explain that in this sense 'every ideology is "pure" appearance, useless, stupid, etc.'. His own preferences emerge by contrast in the insistence that ideology 'must be analyzed historically, in terms of the philosophy of praxis as a superstructure'. From such a standpoint the fact that 'the bad sense of the word has become widespread' is unfortunate: the effect is that 'the theoretical analysis of the concept of ideology has been modified and denatured'.[36] This discussion is interesting in a number of ways. There is, in the first place, the implication that 'the bad sense' was not something integral to Marxist philosophy from the beginning, but an aspect of a development that had come to fruition by the time of writing. There is, moreover, the recognition, which is as clear as the cryptic manner of the *Prison Notebooks* allows, of the contrast between the use of the term for epistemological purposes, as denoting 'pure' appearance, and for those of

social theory, in the analysis of a superstructure. Most
significantly perhaps, there is the suggestion that these two
uses cannot easily be held harmoniously together.

Here again one can hardly fail to be struck by the
prophetic and cautionary value of Gramsci's work. Many
later commentators have believed that there is indeed a
problem in reconciling the two kinds of requirement within
the category of ideology. It has been thought that its
epistemological status must carry with it commitments that
will prove embarrassing for the analysts of superstructures
to try to satisfy, and that the same will be true in reverse for
the epistemologists when it comes to fixing social correlates
for their distinctions. Since, as this essay has tried to show,
the association of either set of ambitions with the classical
Marxist view of ideology is a fundamental error, it stands in
no danger from their supposed lack of coherence. Nevertheless, the assumption that it is inescapably involved in some
such tension is widespread inside and outside 'Marxism'.
Thus, one finds Althusser attributing some of the blame for
his earlier 'theoreticism' to the influence of the equivocal
notion of ideology that appears in *The German Ideology*,
'where one and the same term plays two different roles,
designating a philosophical category on the one hand
(illusion, error), and a scientific concept on the other
(formation of the superstructure)'.[37] In view of this, there is
a measure of irony in the fact that some well-disposed critics
find the same equivocation in his own thought, early and
late: 'there is an ongoing coexistence of – and perhaps an
irresolvable tension between – ideology conceived as the
epistemological antithesis to science-in-general and conceived as an intrinsic element of the structure or fabric of
social formations'.[38] The sense of the uneasy relationship
between the social and the epistemological in the classical
Marxist treatment of ideology has been expressed by other
writers within a quite different perspective. Raymond
Williams concludes a discussion of the position of Marx and
Engels by remarking that ' "ideology" then hovers between

"a system of beliefs characteristic of a certain class" and "a system of illusory beliefs – false ideas or false consciousness – which can be contrasted with true or scientific knowledge" ', and he adds: 'This uncertainty was never really resolved.'[39] The difficulty perceived here is dealt with sympathetically by Williams, but in other hands the belief in the unresolved uncertainty supplies the grounds for a wholesale dismissal of the classical Marxist achievement. It may be useful to illustrate this tendency more fully.

A central plank in Martin Seliger's discussion is the attribution to Marx and Engels of a 'restrictive', 'dogmatic', 'pejorative', 'truth-excluding' use of the term 'ideology'; its identification with 'the falsifying presentation of reality'.[40] Its other main plank is the assumption that 'the Marxist theory of ideology . . . embodies the central hypotheses offered by Marxism for the understanding of social life'.[41] The chief vehicle of this understanding on Seliger's account is a social determinism which is constantly assumed, though never satisfactorily defined. Ideology is said to be identified by Marxism with socially determined consciousness,[42] and the specific agent of the determination is variously acknowledged as 'class', 'class interests', 'class structure', and 'economic and social conditions (and the relationship between them)'.[43] He then tries to show that the two planks will not fit neatly together; that, for instance, it is 'untenable to identify ideology with distorted consciousness and to ascribe it to the belief system of a certain class alone'.[44] He further argues that the tension between the epistemological commitment and the requirements of social explanation was felt by the founders themselves: 'it is safe to assume that Marx could not abide by his dogmatic conception of ideology, because he believed in the possibility of an adequate social science, his social science, and thus found it difficult to judge all existing social science, let alone the natural sciences, in terms of a falsified and falsifying superstructure'.[45] Hence it is that one has to allow for constant, thought always unacknowledged, 'deviations' from the official doctrine on the part of both Marx and Engels. The process of drawing it 'into the orbit of an empirically tenable theory of ideology' was continued by Lukács, again without any acknowledgment of the significance of what was taking place.[46] In the meantime, Lenin, under the pressures of practical needs, had broken completely with the dogmatic sense, and begun to speak of ideology in an 'inclusive', 'non-pejorative' way.[47] This too was accomplished without any hint that the original doctrine was being abandoned. Thus, the picture that emerges of the classical Marxist treatment of ideology is of a medley of disparate elements, given a semblance of unity by the bland assumption or dogmatic assertion of loyalty and continuity, but inherently liable to fly apart at the touch of analysis.

It will by now be clear that every important element in this picture is misconceived. At the heart of it is the familiar, gratuitous assumption that classical Marxism identifies ideology with 'the falsifying presentation of reality'. Moreover, the suggestion that the theory of ideology embodies its central hypotheses for understanding social life involves a gross error of scale, which flows in this case from the particular mistaken belief that that it also seeks to identify ideology with socially determined consciousness. As classical Marxism is involved in neither of these identifications, it escapes the difficulties of trying to reconcile them, and attacks on them, whether they are taken singly or together, leave it wholly unscathed. What must be emphasized here is that one is dealing not with figments of an individual imagination but with representative features of a whole climate of misunderstanding that has come to envelop Marxist and non-Marxist commentators alike. The exemplary point of Seliger's discussion lies just in the way it manages to crystallize so many significant kinds of error and confusion. An attempt has been made in this chapter to suggest the outlines of an explanation of how such a climate could develop in the course of the transition to post-classical Marxism. A great deal of work remains to be done in order to arrive at a fully satisfactory account. For the present one can only insist on the need to dispel the fog, so as to allow the true shape of an important area of intellectual history to be apprehended.

For Marxists the task is yet more pressing, if they are to achieve an adequate sense of the resources afforded by their intellectual inheritance and of the continuing responsibilities it imposes. When the fog is lifted it becomes possible to see that the classical treatment of ideology has an austere kind of continuity. It emerges as a concept with a simple, coherent structure and a limited, though strategic, role in the theory of class struggle. That body of theory is itself central to a Marxist understanding of pre-socialist societies. As such it has constantly to be reviewed in the light of the lessons of praxis. In every historical conjuncture the questions arise of what precisely it has to offer, of how it needs to be developed or modified, and of what can be sustained of the spirit of rational optimism in which it was originally framed. Such questions have as much urgency as ever at the present time. An unfortunate consequence of the systematic distortion surrounding the topic of ideology is that it tends to mask their significance, and makes it harder for them to be posed in complete clarity. Nevertheless, they constitute, together with the more specifically philosophical question highlighted earlier in this discussion of the precise nature of the materialist dialectic, a large part of the programme confronting Marxist thought.

This might be described as a programme of a return to origins; one whose character is fixed by the problems that continue to be posed by the classical literature. Hence, it would be appropriate for attempts to implement it to take their starting points directly from the creators of that literature. Above all, it should involve a return to Marx, still the least understood of those figures. This essay has tried to show something of the resources of his thought, but in philosophy its fertilizing power has hardly begun to be seriously exploited. It is a situation which is due, in part, to the fact that it has so seldom received the kind of patient, rational exegesis given to other major thinkers as a matter of course. It seems natural to suppose that in the context of Britain the attempt to improve matters should be able to make some use of insights and achievements of the linguistic and analytical tradition. The practice of scrupulous, detailed inquiry is, after all, often thought to be its stock-in-trade. Besides, in some areas the issue of relevance is in little doubt: the student of dialectic can hardly afford to ignore its work in the philosophy of logic and of mind and action. A naïve observer might even suppose that from the standpoint of that tradition Marx would appear as a not wholly uncongenial figure. Some qualities in his thought may suggest a curious kind of affinity; as, for instance, its love of the concrete and antipathy to metaphysical speculation, its sceptical realism and caution about exceeding the resources of the argument. Even such less attractive features as the relentless verbal wrangling of the earlier, polemical works do not tell against the suggestion. In fact, of course, little fruitful interaction has taken place: relations have been marked on each side by hostility or condescension. It is true that Marxists can hardly be blamed if the virtues of the analytical school have not been clearly visible to them. For it has consistently turned its least attractive face in their direction. This is in part a consequence of the general tendency for the 'linguistic analysts', in considering the ideas of a philosopher of the past, 'to argue with this dead figure as if he were a colleague in their common-room'.[48] Such egalitarianism has its risks. As the simile suggests, it takes for granted that the argument is, so to speak, always conducted on the analysts' home ground, and their inter-locutor may suffer the complete loss of the context on which his individuality depends. Instead of a living exchange, one then gets a monologue aimed at a ghost. Moreover, the official dispensing with the need for any discipline of historical imagination may tend to leave the analysts at the mercy of their preconceptions. It is, at any rate, true that some of the greatest figures in the history of thought have fared badly in these common-room encounters.[49] Marx hardly seems the most suitable of guests, and the commentaries on his work produced in the analytical tradition have indeed been marked by failure to respect its independent reality, or to come to terms with its self-conception of its existence, even as a prelude to rejection. They have suffered, that is to say, from the lack of a kind of basic seriousness that their undertaking requires. The consequences are pervasive and corrupting, and have been felt not least in a slipshod approach to matters of elementary scholarship.[50] In addition, one has occasionally to acknowledge the presence of an animus derived from objectives that are ideological in the sense with which this essay has been concerned. The consequence of all this is that some of the most widely-canvassed of such works are virtually worthless as commentaries on Marx. This failure has been obvious to thinkers who regard themselves as Marxists, and have some acquaintance with the power and solidity of his thought from the inside. Unfortunately, their rejection of the analytical movement has all too often led to an isolation from all practice of philosophy as such in this country, and thus from what is at least a potentially valuable source of techniques and controls. Instead there has developed a field of 'Marxist theory', with its own conventions governing significance and accomplishment. This is a natural response to a hostile environment, and it has allowed much interesting work to be done. But there has been a price to be paid. The autonomous character of the development has tended to go together with the sense of an audience exclusively of the converted. These circumstances have encouraged some strange forms of self-indulgence on the part of the theorists; a wilfulness in argument, at times even a certain deliberate outrageousness, qualities whose natural affinity is with quite other tendencies in the history of thought than classical Marxism. Moreover, the practice of autonomy works, as one might expect, so as to close the enterprise off from the mainstream of intellectual life: it means in effect the giving up of any ambition to take part in a hegemonic contest; that is, to engage fully in the class struggle in the field of theory. What does emerge is then in danger of being merely a hothouse growth, an exotic kept alive by artificially recreating the conditions of other climates. The will and resources needed for this can hardly be sustained indefinitely. The theory must be naturalized if it is to survive with any vigour, and in doing so it will have to enter into a critical and creative relationship with native strains of thought. Some of the omens for this now seem to be favourable, but it must be admitted that in philosophy the process of getting Marx to speak English has a long way to go.

NOTES

Chapter 1

1 *Selections from the Prison Notebooks of Antonio Gramsci*, edited and translated by Q. Hoare and G. Nowell Smith, London, 1971, (hereafter referred to as SPN), p. 382.
2 *Loc. cit.*
3 SPN, pp. 383-84.
4 It may be helpful to cite some sources for the examples in this paragraph:
  'republican ideology', K. Marx, *The Class Struggles in France 1848-1850*, Moscow, 1972, (hereafter referred to as CSF), p. 51.
  'Hegelian ideology', K. Marx and F. Engels, *The German Ideology*, London, 1965, (hereafter referred to as GI), p. 199.
  'political ideology', GI, p. 40. 'ideology of the bourgeoisie', GI, p. 194.
  'his (the political economists') ideology' K. Marx, *Capital*, Vol (i), London, 1974 (hereafter referred to as Cap(i)), p. 716.
  'ideological expression', GI, p. 190.
  'ideological forms', K. Marx, *A Contribution to the Critique of Political Economy*, Moscow, 1970, (hereafter referred to as CCPE), p. 21.
  'ideological phrases', GI, p. 579.
  'ideological conceptions', Cap(i),p.352,n.2.
  'ideological contempt', GI, p. 336.
  'ideological theory', GI, p. 580.
  'the ideoligical stand point', K. Marx, *Grundrisse*, London, 1973 p. 164.
  'ideological reflexes and echoes', GI, p. 38.
  'ideological nonsense', K. Marx, *Critique of the Gotha Programme*, Moscow, 1971, p. 18.
  'ideological distortion', GI, p. 474.
  'ideological method', GI, p. 514.

Napoleon's 'scorn of *ideologists*', K. Marx and F. Engels, *The Holy Family*, Moscow, 1975, (hereafter referred to as HF), p. 146.
'the Young Hegelian ideologists', GI, p. 30.
'the *ideological cretins* of the bourgeoisie', K. Marx and F. Engels, *Articles from the Neue Rheinische Zeitung 1848-49*, Moscow, 1972, (hereafter referred to as ANRZ), p. 189.
'the ideological representatives and spokesmen', CSF, p. 28.
'the "ideological" classes', Cap(i), p. 420.
'the capitalist and his ideological representative', Cap (i), p. 537, (or simply 'the capitalist and his ideologist', *der Kapitalist und sein Ideolog*, see K. Marx-F. Engels, *Werke*, Berlin, 1956ff., Vol 23, p. 598.).
'the abstract ideas of ideology', GI, p. 260.
'ideological postulate', GI, p. 517.
'ideological system', K. Marx, *The Poverty of Philosophy*, Moscow, 1955, (hereafter referred to as PP), p. 96.
'ideological formula', CSF, p. 102.
'ideologically disinterested names', CSF, p. 103.
'ideological manifestoes', K. Marx and F. Engels, *Selected Correspondence*, Moscow, n.d., (hereafter referred to as MESC), p. 69.
5   CCPE, p. 21.
6   CSF, p. 103.
7   CSF, pp. 50-51.
8   SPN, p. 200.
9   GI, p. 29.
10 GI, p. 30.
11 GI, p. 30.
12 GI, p. 231.
13 GI, p. 429.
14 PP, p. 105.
15 See, e.g., GI, p. 23.
16 HF, Ch. 6, Section 3(d).
17 Cap(i), p. 24.
18 Cap(i), p. 25.
19 ANRZ, p. 142.
20 Cap(i), p. 77.
21 *Loc. cit.*
22 Cap(i), p. 83.
23 Cap(i), pp. 83-84.
24 On the general significance of analogy see, e.g., *The Savage Mind*, London, 1972, (hereafter referred to as SM), p. 263. The same point is made in M. Godelier, *Perspectives in Marxist Anthropology*, Cambridge, 1977, p. 182: 'Analogy is the general principle organising

the representation of the world in and through primitive thinking.' This part of Godelier's work is an illuminating discussion of the lessons of anthropology for ideological analysis. It is so in spite of his conforming to a definition of ideology as 'the sphere of illusory representations of the real', (p. 181). On this issue see below, Ch.3.

25   C. Lévi-Strauss, *Totemism*, London, 1962, (hereafter referred to as Tot), p. 85.

26   Tot, p. 63.

27   Tot, p. 89.

28   Tot, p. 91.

29   SM, p. 161.

30   Tot, p. 88.

31   Tot, p. 90.

32   Tot, p. 40.

33   Tot, p. 41.

34   Tot, p. 42.

35   Tot, p. 101.

36   SM, p. 115.

37   SM, p. 123.

38   It is, of course, Wittgenstein's 'general form of propositions', *Tractatus Logico –Philosophicus* 4.5. See, e.g., translation by D. F. Pears and B. F. McGuinness, London, 1961, (hereafter referred to as TLP), p. 70 and p. 71.

39   *From Max Weber: Essays in Sociology*, translated, edited and with an introduction by H. H. Gerth and C. Wright Mills, London, 1948, p. 62.

40   M. Weber, *Gesammelte Aufsätze zur Religionssoziologie*, Vol(i), Tübingen, 1920, p. 83. The translation here follows that of Talcott Parsons, in *The Protestant Ethic and the Spirit of Capitalism*, New York, 1958, (hereafter referred to as PESP), p. 91; except that Parsons renders *Wahlverwandschaften*, ('elective affinities'), as 'correlations' and, in the next sentence, as 'relationships'.

41   PESP, e.g., p. 64.

42   L. Goldmann, *The Hidden God*, London, 1964, (hereafter referred to as HG), p. 120.

43   HG, p. 50.

Chapter 2

1   Many instances might be cited; e.g., 'According to Marx and Engels "ideologies" were false thinking determined by class interests . . .'. (H. B. Acton, *The Illusion of the Epoch*, London, 1955, p. 132). This formulation is noteworthy in capturing so many of the basic

misconceptions with which the present essay is concerned. On the views of Engels and the question of 'false thinking' see below, Ch.3.

2   GI, p. 194.
3   GI, p. 214.
4   CCPE, p. 21.
5   GI, p. 233.
6   GI, p. 460.
7   See above Ch. 1, n. 18.
8   K. Marx, *Theories of Surplus Value*, Part Two, London, 1969, (hereafter referred to as TSV (ii)), p. 118.
9   TSV(ii), p. 119.
10 TSV(ii), p. 120.
11 See, e.g., *Theories of Surplus Value*, Part Three, London, 1972; Subject Index, references under 'Ricardo, David – argues from the standpoint of developed capitalist production'.
12 See, e.g., TSV(ii), p. 153.
13 TSV(ii), p. 118.
14 PP, p. 150.
15 K. Marx, *The Eighteenth Brumaire of Louis Bonaparte*, Moscow, 1934, (hereafter referred to as EB), p. 106.
16 V. I. Lenin, *What is to be Done?* Moscow, 1947, (hereafter referred to as WD), p. 69.
17 WD, p. 31.
18 WD, p. 39.
19 WD, p. 41.
20 WD, p. 45.
21 See, e.g., Ch. 3, n.55; Ch. 4, n. 47
22 WD, p. 40.
23 WD, p. 41.
24 G. Lukács, *History and Class Consciousness*, London, 1971, (hereafter referred to as HCC), p. 51.
25 HCC, p. XVIII.
26 As the translator's note makes clear; HCC, pp. 344-45. For confirmation in the text see, e.g., p. 52, p. 58.
27 HCC, p. 46.
28 HF, p. 45.
29 On this point see the discussion by István Mészáros in I. Mészáros (ed), *Aspects of History and Class Consciousness*, London, 1971. It argues that 'Lukács's distinction between "ascribed" and "psychological" class consciousness is a reformulation of one of the basic tenets of the Marxian system', and that 'it is quite impossible to make sense of Marx's theory of classes and class consciousness without this vital distinction'. (p. 94).
30 HCC, p. 65.

31 For these references see, e.g., in sequence, pp. 10,32,36, 36,67,80,227, and 59.

32 HCC, p. 228.

33 HCC, pp. 258-59.

34 N. Poulantzas, *Political Power and Social Classes*, London, 1973, (hereafter referred to as PPSC), p. 205.

35 G. Stedman Jones, 'The Marxism of the Early Lukács: an Evaluation', *New Left Review*, 70, November-December 1971, pp. 27-64, (hereafter referred to as MEL), reprinted in *Western Marxism A Critical Reader*, edited by New Left Review, London, 1977, pp. 11-60.

36 MEL, p. 48.

37 MEL, p. 49.

38 MEL, p. 50.

39 HCC, p. 44.

40 HCC, p. 208.

41 HCC, p. 275.

42 HCC, p. 276.

43 HCC, p. 76.

44 HCC, p. 71.

45 HCC, p. 74.

46 HCC, p. 304. See also pp. 79,228,305,310,312,314,330.

47 HCC, p. 67.

48 HCC, p. 36.

49 '*aus eigenen Kräften ihre Position ideologisch zu verteidigen*', G. Lukács, *Werke*, Frühschriften (ii), Band(ii), Neuwied, 1968, p. 403. HCC writes of 'defending its own position ideologically and with its own resources'. (p. 227)

50 HCC, p. 227.

51 HCC, p. 67.

52 HCC, p. 227.

53 MEL, p. 49.

54 See above n.18 and n.19.

55 PPSC, e.g., p. 206

56 PPSC, p. 207.

57 PPSC, p. 198.

58 PPSC, p. 207.

59 PPSC, pp. 208-09.

60 In support of this interpretation see, e.g., pp. 73,75,209,282.

61 HCC, p. 77.

62 On this point see, e.g., p. 146 and p. 173.

63 HCC, pp. XVIII-XIX.

64 HCC, p.XXXIII.

65 HCC, pp. XVIII, XXV, XXVII.

66   HCC, p. 259. For another typical expression see p. 70: ' "Ideology" for the proletariat is no banner to follow into battle, nor is it a cover for its true objectives: it is the objective and the weapon itself.'

67   HCC, p.XXIII.

68   HCC, p. 68.

69   HCC, p. 70.

70   HCC, p. 224.

71   PPSC, p. 206.

72   *Working Papers in Cultural Studies 10*, 'On Ideology', Birmingham, 1977, (hereafter referred to as WPCS), is a collection which illustrates this clearly.

73   L. Althusser, *For Marx*, London, 1969, (hereafter referred to as FM). L. Althusser and E. Balibar, *Reading Capital*, London, 1970, (hereafter referred to as RC). L. Althusser, 'Ideology and Ideological State Apparatuses', *Lenin and Philosophy and other essays*, London, 1971, (hereafter referred to as LP). L. Althusser, *Essays in Self-Criticism*, London, 1976, (hereafter referred to as ESC).

74   FM, p. 69.

75   RC, p. 52.

76   RC, p. 53.

77   See the discussion in T. S. Kuhn, *The Structure of Scientific Revolutions*, Chicago, 1962.

78   FM, p. 231.

79   LP, p. 152.

80   LP, p. 160.

81   FM, p. 232.

82   *Loc. cit.*

83   FM, p. 235.

84   LP, p. 160.

85   LP, p. 169.

86   FM, p. 234.

87   LP, p. 156.

88   FM, p. 235.

89   LP, pp. 164-65.

90   CCPE, p. 189.

91   See, e.g., J. Rancière, 'On the theory of ideology', *Radical Philosophy*, 7, Spring 1974, and A. Callinicos, *Althusser's Marxism*, London, 1976, esp. pp. 96-101.

92   To put the point in this way is to accept what has been called 'the most widespread criticism' of the essay on 'Ideology and Ideological State Apparatuses', that it offers an account 'in which class struggle is almost entirely absent', and, hence, to accept that the 'rhetorical invocation of the class struggle in the Afterword' is indeed 'an ill-disguised apology for absences in the text'. (WPCC, p. 97). The

view taken in ESC is that on the role of class struggle the position adopted in LP 'was still an improvised solution, that is, a semi-compromise'. (ESC, p. 150). It may be that Althusser's thinking was then in a process of change and that in some respects LP should be regarded as 'a work of the break'. But so far as our present interests are concerned it fits most naturally, as the discussion has tried to show, with the earlier work, and taken together the results present a sharp contrast with the views of ESC.

93 ESC, e.g., pp. 37,39,58,72,142,166.
94 ESC, p. 130.
95 ESC, p. 146.
96 ESC, p. 148.
97 ESC, p. 141.
98 ESC, p. 179.
99 ESC, p. 177, p. 175.
100 ESC, p. 177.
101 *Loc. cit.*
102 ESC, pp. 49-50.
103 ESC, p. 119.
104 ESC, p. 106.
105 ESC, p. 155.
106 ESC, p. 55.
107 ESC, p. 201.
108 See ESC, p. 165.
109 See, e.g., J. Ranciére, *op cit.*, and A. Callinicos, *op cit.*
110 ESC. See esp. n.19, p. 124.
111 ESC. pp. 147-48.
112 For examples, see pp. 126, 151,157.
113 ESC. p. 116.
114 ESC, pp. 78-79.
115 ESC. p. 173.
116 ESC. p. 157.
117 ESC. p. 160.

Chapter 3

1 Ch. 1 above, n.5.
2 K. Marx and F. Engels, *The Communist Manifesto*, London, 1967, (hereafter referred to as CM), p. 91.
3 SPN, p. 162n.
4 This has been noticed by W. L. McBride: 'it is surprisingly difficult to extract from any section of it a straightforward exposition of its supposedly central term, "ideology", that is at all adequate in length

or detail'. 'Nevertheless', he goes on, 'the authors' basic insight is comparatively easy to reconstruct.' He confidently proceeds to reconstruct it in terms of a familiar combination of pejorative connotation and social determinism. (*The Philosophy of Marx*, London, 1977, pp. 71-75). This example is interesting in showing the grip of the conventional wisdom on a writer who has an inkling of the uncertainty of its foundations.

5   GI, p. 61.

6   GI, p. 77.

7   GI, p. 417.

8   See, e.g., in sequence, pp. 194,474,473.

9   See, e.g., in sequence, pp. 580,517,514,186.

10   GI, p. 37.

11   GI, p. 29.

12   *Die Deutsche Ideologie*, Berlin, 1960, (hereafter referred to as DI), p. 22. I am indebted to Herbert Scheidt, to Juliane Signist and to colleagues at the Polytechnic of the South Bank for help with the translation of this sentence.

13   The same rendering is given in Vol. 5 of Marx-Engels, *Collected Works,* London, 1967, p. 36, and in *Writings of the Young Marx on Philosophy and Society*, edited and translated by L. D. Easton and K. H. Guddat, New York, 1967, p. 414.

14   HF, p. 226. Cap (1), p. 29. GI, p. 145.

15   See *Hegel Texts and Commentary*, translated and edited by W. Kaufmann, New York, 1966, pp. 40-42 and n. 9, p. 43.

16   For the use of the clause as an unconditional assertion see, e.g., M. Evans, *Karl Marx*, London, 1975, p. 82.

17   See above, pp. 15-16.

18   This essay has hitherto spoken of Marx alone in connection with these works. If this practice is found seriously objectionable, it can be given up without affecting the main point. That concerns the need to distinguish between an opinion advanced by Engels in old age and all the other expressions of his position and that of Marx. See the discussion following.

19   EB, p. 9.

20   K. Marx and F. Engels, *Selected Works*, Vol(ii), Moscow, 1958, (hereafter referred to as MESW), pp. 398-99.

21   MESW, p. 399.

22   MESW, p. 400.

23   AD, p. 116.

24   A division apparently resented in this instance by Engels. See his letter to Marx of May 28, 1876: 'It's all very well for you to talk. You can lie warm in bed and study ground rent in general and Russian agrarian conditions in particular with nothing to disturb you – but I am

to sit on the hard bench, swill cold wine, suddenly interrupt everything again and get after the scalp of the boring Dühring.' MESC, p. 371.

25 AD, p. 49.

26 Perhaps the nadir of scholarship in this field is reached in John Plamenatz's assertion that 'Marx often called ideology "false consciousness". ' *Ideology*, London, 1971, p. 23. Naturally no sources are cited in support, This assertion has also been noted in M. Seliger, *The Marxist Conception of Ideology*, Cambridge, 1977, (hereafter referred to as MCI), p. 31.

27 MESC, p. 541.

28 See Ch. 2, n.74.

29 This formulation is chosen simply because it is representative and succinct. It is said to be what 'ideology' signifies 'in the use that Karl Marx gave it' in the entry on 'Ideology' by David Braybrooke, in *The Encyclopaedia of Philosophy*, Paul Edwards, editor in chief, New York and London, 1967, Vol 4, pp. 124-25.

30 MESC, p. 551.

31 See Ch. 2, n.82.

32 HCC, p. 7.

33 HCC, p. 130.

34 HCC, p. 233.

35 HCC, p. 131.

36 HCC, p. 213, n.32.

37 HCC, p. 47.

38 HCC, p. 257.

39 HCC, p.1X.

40 HCC, p. 192.

41 HCC, p. 24, n.6; HCC, p. 207. For Lukács's change of mind on this see HCC, p.XVI.

42 HCC, p. 10.

43 HCC, p. 27.

44 HCC, p. 148.

45 *'Bildhaftigkeit der Gedanken'*, *Philosophische Grammatik*, Oxford, 1969, p. 163. The phrase is translated as in the text in A. Kenny, *Wittgenstein*, London, 1973, p. 224.

46 HCC, p. 114.

47 See, e.g., HCC, pp. 102-03.

48 TLP, 6.45, 6.41, 7.

49 HCC, p. 120.

50 L. Wittgenstein, *Philosophical Investigations*, Oxford, 1963, p. 226.

51 Some remarks made by Lukács many years later demonstrate both his interest in the particular topic of this discussion and his respect for Wittgenstein. 'Take on the other hand a system of ideas such as

neo-positivism which restricts the whole world to a manipulated rationality and rejects everything that would transgress this limit. Now originally neo-positivism had a real thinker as one of its founders, namely Wittgenstein who founded the neo-positivist positions really philosophically, saw quite clearly that on the margin of their positions, if I might put it this way, there lay a desert of irrationalism about which nothing rational could be said from the neo-positivist standpoint. Wittgenstein, however, was much too intelligent to believe that the world beyond the statements of positivism did not exist, and on the margin of Wittgenstein's philosophy there is, I believe, a terrain of irrationality – this is not simply my own observation but one that many others have made.' *Conversations with Lukács*, edited by T. Pinkus, Cambridge, Mass., 1975, p. 48.

52   LP, p. 150.

53   See, e.g., J. Mepham, 'The Theory of Ideology in Capital', *Radical Philosophy*, no. 2, Summer, 1972.

54   'Marxism has won its historic significance as the ideology of the revolutionary proletariat because . . .'. V. I. Lenin, *Selected Works*, Moscow, 1968, (hereafter referred to as LSW) p. 616. For Lukács, see Ch. 2 above, n. 33.

55   Thus, for instance, in agreeing with E. H. Carr's judgment that 'in Marx "ideology" is a negative term', whereas in Lenin, ' "ideology" becomes neutral or positive', Martin Seliger comments: 'It is not surprising that Lenin offered no explanation for his drastic change of the use of the term, since he did not, to my knowledge, confess to this change in the first place. (And the same seems to apply to Lukács.)' MCI, p. 83. This difficulty dissolves once it is realized that no change occurred which Lenin or Lukács needed to confess.

56   GI, p. 62.

57   CM, p. 92.

58   'A Contribution to the Critique of Hegel's Philosophy of Right. Introduction', *Early Writings*, London, 1975, (hereafter referred to as MEW) p. 256.

59   GI, p. 87.

60   MEW, p. 256.

61   K. Marx, *Economic and Philosophic Manuscripts of 1844*, Moscow, 1974, p. 73.

62   GI, p. 94.

63   HCC, p. 174. For the original remarks see MEW, p. 415.

64   Quoted in *Karl Marx, Selected Writings in Sociology and Social Philosophy*, edited by T. B. Bottomore and M. Rubel, London, 1963, p. 210.

65   GI, p. 96.

66 LSW, p. 604.

67 HCC, p. 163.

68 MESC, p. 86.

69 K. Marx, *Theories of Surplus Value*, Part 1, London, 1969, p. 40.

70 Cap(i), p. 483.

71 Cap(i), p. 49.

72 See Ch. 1, n.18.

73 HCC, p. 73.

74 Ch. 2, n.17.

75 See Ch. 2. n.18, n.19, n.22, n.23 and the discussion corresponding.

76 HCC, p. 224.

77 K. Marx, 'Theses on Feuerbach', See GI, pp. 661, 667 and DI, p. 585.

78 HCC, p. 123.

79 HCC, p. 145.

80 HCC, p. 146.

81 HCC, p. 81. A postscript to the discussion is once again provided by Wittgenstein: 'The sickness of a time is cured by an alteration in the mode of life of human beings, and it was possible for the sickness of philosophical problems to get cured only through a changed mode of thought and of life, not through a medicine invented by an individual.' *Remarks on the Foundations of Mathematics*, Oxford, 1967, p. 57e.

82 See Ch. 2, n.67, and the discussion corresponding.

83 HCC, p. XXIII.

84 Thus, for instance, the duality of thought and being is said to be 'only a special case' of it. HCC, p. 123.

85 Ch. 2, n.66.

86 Ch. 2, n.69.

87 HCC, p. 76.

88 V. I. Lenin, 'A Letter to the Northern League', *Collected Works*, London, Vol 6, p. 163.

Chapter 4

1 P. Anderson, *Considerations on Western Marxism*, London, 1976, (hereafter referred to as CWM).

2 CWM, p. 29.

3 *Loc. cit.*

4 CWM, pp. 29-30.

5 CWM, p. 31.

6 CWM, p. 42.

7 CWM, p. 42-43.

8 HCC, p. XIII.

9   See, e.g., Lucien Goldmann's essay 'Reflections on *History and Class Consciousness*' in I. Mészáros, (ed), *op. cit.*, p. 69, and G. H. R. Parkinson, *Georg Lukács*, London, 1977, p. 7.

10 See above, p. 57.

11 CWM, pp. 7-8, 25-26.

12 CWM, p. 92.

13 CWM, pp. 32-34.

14 CWM, p. 49.

15 CWM, p. 93. See also pp. 52-53 and pp. 91-92, n.40.

16 CWM, p. 75.

17 CWM, p. 55.

18 CWM, pp. 44-45.

19 CWM, p. 45.

20 CWM, p. 75.

21 The key text here is Karl Mannheim's *Ideologie und Utopie*, Bonn, 1929; published in English with additional material as *Ideology and Utopia*, London, 1936.

22 FM. pp. 231-36. See above. pp. 66-72, pp. 97-99.

23 CWM, see pp. 72,81,91.

24 CWM, pp. 101-06,113-21.

25 Perhaps the most striking use of such categories is in the argument purporting to show that the traditional understanding of 'the unity of theory and practice' needs to be qualified:

> If the proper designation for Marxism is historical materialism, it must be – above all – a theory of history. Yet history is – pre-eminently – the past . . . The past, which cannot be amended or undone, can be known with greater certainty than the present, whose actions have yet to be done, and there is more of it. There will thus always remain an inherent scissiparity between knowledge and action, theory and practice, for any possible science of history.

CWM, pp. 109-10. It is of course true that the traditional view cannot be sustained unless it is understood as a specifically dialectical unity that is in question. The function of the dialectic is precisely to dissolve such abstract oppositions as that of 'the past' and 'the present' here. It would also, incidentally, act as a safeguard against the kind of ingenuousness that is displayed. Anderson labels his objection 'insuperable', and adds: 'It is strange that it has not been made more frequently before.'(CWM, p. 109). No doubt Lukács goes too far in defining 'orthodox Marxism' solely in terms of allegiance to the dialectical method, independently of any commitment to substantive theses (HCC, p. 1). The present case illustrates the opposite kind of danger, in showing that a radical conscience and an eye for the social determinants of ideas do not suffice to constitute a Marxist historiography.

26 CWM, p. 67. This point is acceptable so far as it goes, but a full discussion would have to take account of the importance for

Gramsci of the idea that 'the real philosopher is, and cannot be other than, the politician, the active man who modifies the environment, understanding by environment the *ensemble* of relations which each of us enters to take part in'. SPN, p. 352.

27 CWM, p. 54.
28 CWM, p. 77.
29 CWM, p. 78.
30 See, e.g., SPN, p. 175, n.75 and text corresponding.
31 SPN, pp. 388,432,433.
32 See above, pp. 6-7.
33 SPN, p. 328.
34 See above, p. 54.
35 SPN, p. 164.
36 SPN, p. 376.
37 ESC, p. 119.
38 WPCS, p. 103.
39 R. Williams, *Marxism and Literature*, Oxford, 1977, p. 66.
40 MCI, See, e.g., pp. 3,7,8,10,87. This point is not developed with much care or consistency by Seliger, and is sometimes stated in what seem to be gratuitously extreme forms. Thus at one point 'Marx and Engels's dogmatic conception of ideology' is said to require that one 'go on insisting that as a matter of principle all consciousness is false consciousness', (p. 81). Elsewhere he seems to take the 'false consciousness' thesis as implying that ideology is constituted solely by propositional elements, each one of which has the truth value of falsity. See p. 142.
41 MCI, p. 202.
42 MCI, p. 76.
43 See, in sequence, pp. 77,7 and 157,166,126.
44 MCI, p. 22.
45 MCI, p. 143.
46 MCI, p. 118.
47 MCI, p. 107. See also pp. 81-94.
48 This description is from a discussion between Bryan Magee and Bernard Williams, *The Listener*, 9.3.78, p. 299. Its accuracy is accepted by Williams who goes on to defend the value of such an approach.
49 There is not space to document this fully here and, in any case, the worst excesses are now in the past. Something of the atmosphere of the common-room in those days is caught in the following anecdote by Anthony Kenny: 'Some fifteen years ago I was invited by a publisher to write a textbook on Descartes. I was disinclined to do so. "Why do a book on Descartes?" I said to a friend who was a senior philosopher. "He writes well enough, but you could put his main

ideas on the back of a postcard, and they are all wrong. He would not repay the effort of working through his writings." ' *The Times Higher Educational Supplement*, 14.4.78., p. 185. Fuller documentation is provided in a work in the 'Philosophy Now' series, *Philosophy and its Past*, by J. Rée, M. Ayers and A. Westoby, Hassocks, 1978.

50   Some examples should be given here. For Plamenatz, see Ch. 3, n.26. Egregious instances also occur in the writings of Karl Popper, perhaps the critic of Marx most admired within the analytical movement. Thus, in the anxiety to prove Marx an 'historicist', he cites the statement of the aim of *Capital* as being 'to lay bare the economic law of motion of human society', where the actual text reads 'modern' for 'human'. (*The Poverty of Historicism*, London, 1961, p. 49. See Cap(i), p. 20). One should also note the ruthless use of selective quotations for the same end. Thus, he refers to the statement of 'the absolute general law of capitalist accumulation', while omitting the qualification that immediately follows it: 'Like all other laws it is modified in its working by many circumstances, the analysis of which does not concern us here.' (*The Open Society and its Enemies*, vol(ii), London, 1952, p. 186. Cap(i), p. 603) See the discussion of these examples in W. A. Suchting, 'Marx, Popper, and "Historicism" ', *Inquiry*, 15, Autumn, 1972, pp. 235-66.

INDEX